email libra
Internet

Integrated Business Continuity:
Maintaining Resilience in Uncertain Times

Integrated Business Continuity:
Maintaining Resilience in Uncertain Times

By Geary W. Sikich

Copyright © 2003 by
PennWell Corporation
1421 South Sheridan Road
Tulsa, Oklahoma 74112-6600 USA

800.752.9764
+1.918.831.9421
sales@pennwell.com
www.pennwell.com
www.pennwell-store.com

Book design by Amy Spehar
Cover design by Clark Bell

Library of Congress Cataloging-in-Publication Data
Sikich, Geary W.
    Integrated Business Continuity: Maintaining Resilience in
Uncertain Times / by Geary W. Sikich.
        p. cm.
Includes index.
    ISBN 0-87814-865-5
    1. Crisis management. 2. Emergency management. 3.
Business planning. I. Title.
    HD49 .S557 2003
    658.4'056--dc21

                                            2002152121

Printed in the United States of America

1   2   3   4   5   07   06   05   04   03

Dedication

This book is dedicated to the visionaries, those unique individuals who are not afraid to speak out and let their voices be heard. These are the individuals who embrace change and see it as a challenge, an opportunity, not a disruption of the status quo. To those who, when they are told, "It can't be done" find a way to get it done, I offer you this text. You are willing to see things from a different perspective, and often take the unpopular path because it is the right thing to do. To those who have taken the chance and learned not to repeat their mistakes, I hope this text stirs your interest and pushes you to look anew.

To these individuals, these creative thinkers, who tinker and are inspired by their restlessness to get out, seek, explore, and find new challenges, I wish you speed on your journey. To all of us who look at life as an adventure and a journey without end, I dedicate this book.

There are many who assisted me with the refinement of the thoughts that I have turned into the pages of this book to whom I wish to express my thanks. Specifically, I want to thank my colleagues, Michael Huggins, Brian Meyers, and Thomas Baines for their contributions and encouragement in pushing me to complete this text. And of course, to my sons, Aaron and Drake, thanks for being yourselves. To all of you, thanks and good reading.

INITIATING A NEW ORDER OF THINGS

"It must be considered that there is nothing more difficult to carry out, nor more doubtful of success, nor more dangerous to handle, than to initiate a new order of things. For the reformer has enemies in all those who would profit by the old order, and only lukewarm defenders in all those who would profit by the new order. This lukewarmness arising partly from the fear of their adversaries, who have the laws in their favor; and partly from the incredulity of mankind, who do not truly believe in anything new until they have actually experienced it."

—Niccolo Machiavelli - The Prince

Table of Contents

List of Figures

List of Tables

List of Acronyms

BCMP	business continuity management plan
BCMT	business continuity management team
CIO	chief information officer
EEA	Essential Elements of Analysis
EPA	Environmental Protection Agency
EPIP	Event Plan Implementing Procedures
GNP	gross national product
HUMINT	human intelligence
MOE	Measures of Effectiveness
MOP	Measures of Performance
NIPC	National Infrastructure Protection Center
OPEC	Organization of Petroleum Exporting Countries
PBX	Private Branch Exchange
PCO	primary communications objective
RMRO	Response management and recovery objectives
SCADA	Supervisory Control and Data Acquisition (system)
SCIP	Society of Competitive Intelligence Professionals
TCE	Trichloroethylene
UPS	uninterruptible power source
VPN	virtual private networks
WMD	weapons of mass destruction (disruption)

Foreword

As the authors of *Blur* point out:

> *Connectivity, speed and intangible values are the new driving forces in business today. Traditional business boundaries are blurring as everyone becomes electronically connected. The traditional rules governing the conduct of business are blurred as businesses are redefined, products become services, services become products and business lines change constantly.*

As business change accelerates, it is getting more and more difficult for traditional strategists to achieve an accurate focus on the current situation. Strategy, in the traditional sense, is outdated before it can be implemented. Speed, operating at real time, is pushing traditional strategy development, forecasting, competitive intelligence collection, and analysis to new limits. For every organization, vision, mission, and values are important; they shape strategy for the organization. Strategy, in turn, is influenced by information in the form of competitive intelligence; competitive intelligence initiatives seek to fulfill a company's strategy. Due to the speed of business in the modern organization today, "crises"(disruptive events) are prevalent. Every "crisis" is a violation of vision, mission, and values. Every crisis solution demands a modification, if not wholesale reworking, of strategy (vision, mission, values) and competitive intelligence activities. As the strategy and competitive intelligence disciplines come under more scrutiny, the need for a comprehensive event management system becomes paramount. The integration of strategy, competitive intelligence, and event management into a vertically and horizontally seamless process allows for "integrated" business continuity.

An effective and well adhered-to "integrated" business continuity management system provides value for the organization, by allowing it to adapt to the rapidly changing business environment we are faced with today. The speed of response to an event will determine the outcome, either positive or negative, for the organization and its value chain. The ability to connect all the touchpoints within an organization and its value chain during an event is essential for the success of response, management, and recovery efforts. The value achieved through an organized response, management, and recovery effort to a disruptive event is measured by the intangibles—perception, information, relationships, and loyalty. These cannot be seen, and often it is difficult to measure their impact.

All organizations plan for business success, yet few plan for the potentially devastating effects of an event that becomes a "crisis". Fewer still know and understand the critical process of knowledge management. "Crises" can take many forms; being prepared can be the most effective tool you can employ to assure that your business survives. Where's your next event that has potential for becoming a "crisis" coming from? Will it be a time-critical issue that demands immediate action? Will it be a time-sensitive issue that, if not addressed, will erupt into a full-blown "crisis"? Or will it be a time-dependent issue that lingers unnoticed until it's too late to react effectively? No one plans to have a business disruption; we plan for business growth and success.

Disruptive events, small and large, don't make appointments; they can and do occur at any time and under the most unfavorable conditions. You can, however, prepare your organization, have in place early warning systems, and minimize the potential disruption to your business, your life, and your community, by adopting and developing a proactive business continuity process. Incorporating your business continuity process into the way you do business instead of as an adjunct to the business that your organization does can further ensure that your enterprise will be around after an event, instead of as a footnote to the event.

With the tragic events that occurred on Sept. 11, 2001 in New York City, Washington, D.C., and in a field in Pennsylvania, the need to address business survivability in a "new threat environment" has gotten a lot of press. However, is it truly a "new threat environment"? Have we not had the threat of terrorism and acts of violence facing society for some time? The obvious answer is yes, we have. What changed, as a result of Sept. 11, 2001, was not the nature of the threat, but the magnitude. It came to our shores and it occurred on a scale that few could have imagined. We now have many who predict such dire events as a nuclear attack, or chemical and biological attacks, that may affect millions. While these dire predictions may come to pass (hopefully, not), there are things that can be done to lessen the effect and possibly mitigate the event before it occurs. I, therefore, have based much of this book on the following assumptions.

COMPLEXITY—NETWORKS—TOUCHPOINTS

My assumptions for this book, while focusing on business, can be applied to other entities, including government. As such, I have taken the liberty to use the term "business" in the broadest sense of the word and will entrust the reader to substitute the appropriate terminology as applicable when the word "business" is used.

The term "business continuity" as used in this text will refer to an integrated process that combines—

- "life safety" (emergency preparedness, emergency response)
- "disaster recovery" (information/data recovery)
- "business resumption" (facilities/operations recovery)
- "crisis management" (internal/external communications, issues management) under the term
- "event management." Event management is combined with strategy and competitive intelligence initiatives to create an "integrated" approach to business continuity.

I use the term *business continuity* as an integrated approach, based on common terminology, detailed assessment of relationships/touchpoints and integrated response, management, recovery, and information-sharing processes. This integrated process is based on a careful identification, analysis, assessment, and prioritization of the organization's ability to reduce its activities until it reaches stability and to maintain stability as it adds back activities. I will use the terms *graceful degradation* and *agile restoration* throughout this text as I investigate the business continuity process.

By *graceful degradation*, I mean your organization's ability to identify the event and its consequences, and establish minimal stable functionality, *i.e.*, to "devolve" the organization to the most robust, less functional configuration available in the least disruptive manner possible, and to begin to direct initial efforts for rapid restoration of services in a timely fashion. The integrated approach embraces the blending of strategy, competitive intelligence, event management, and consequence management as key driving forces for business continuity.

Businesses (and governmental entities) are complex systems operating within multiple networks. These systems are composed of people, knowledge (often referred to as information and intelligence), strategy, competitive intelligence initiatives, event management capabilities (or lack thereof), relationships and interrelationships, spheres of influence, equipment, and facilities. Simply put, these are physical and non-physical elements.

Each of the elements within a business system has "touchpoints" to other elements within and external to the system. Each touchpoint can present an asset or a threat to the system's survivability.

In order to effectively assess, evaluate, and categorize assets, risks, vulnerabilities, threats, and hazards, all touchpoints within a system, within a given network must be considered to determine effects of potential degradation and the consequences associated with degrees of degradation.

The actions of an organization (substitute company, government, etc.) within its network will be inadequate unless the entire network responds in kind. This evokes the theory that for every action there is a reaction. Today, due to many factors, most organizations lack the resources and specialized skills to know what to do to maximize positive network effects. This is due partially to the fact that most organizations do not consider event management to be an integral part of the business process. Rather, event management is seen as an adjunct to the business and, in some instances, a stopgap measure that is only tacitly addressed.

Most business people have been trained to "solve anticipated events." They have not been "educated" to solve unexpected "problems." For this assumption, I credit Ian Mitroff. Dr. Mitroff has written extensively on the subject of crisis management. As such, his observations regarding training and thought processes should be investigated thoroughly.

If we combine the comments from the authors of *Blur* with these of Dr. Mitroff and the complexity/touchpoint assumption, we understand one of the potential quandries for the business continuity: "How do we blend strategy, competitive intelligence, and event management into an integrated business continuity process?"

Most training exercises conducted today are pre-formulated in such a manner that they have limited scopes and/or very focused solutions. We need to acknowledge that an event in our complex world has many potential issues that are uniquely seen from the perspective of many different and diverse stakeholders. Because the perceptions of real-world problems vary from stakeholder to stakeholder, training exercises need to be refocused to reflect the identification of event triggers—not on anticipated problem solutions. We can be assured that most organizations can resolve an event, given the time and resources.

"Before *real problems* can be solved they must first be *characterized in terms recognizable to all stakeholders*," Dr. Mitroff says (emphasis mine).

I believe the key to characterization is an organization's ability to identify its touchpoints; determine its assets, vulnerabilities, threats, hazards, and risks; and plan for graceful degradation and agile restoration (*i.e.*, integrate strategy, competitive intelligence, and event management). Dr. Mitroff uses the term "critical thinking"—the ability to see problems from multiple perspectives, expose critical underlying assumptions, challenge and reverse one's assumptions, and reformulate basic arguments. He concludes by observing, "Unless one practices critical thinking, one is very likely to commit a very important error: *Solving the wrong problem precisely.*"

Based on earlier assumptions, this book addresses the integration of strategy, competitive intelligence, and event management into an integrated business continuity process. In today's high-availability, high-connectivity environment, the complexity of strategy, competitive intelligence, and event management require this blending to facilitate growth, survival, and resilience. Today, having a business continuity process in place to prevent, respond to, and adjust the course of action of the organization to a variety of calamities that have the potential to create significant business interruption is essential to business survival.

The challenge many companies face is determining what kind of business continuity process should be developed. Many companies will arrive at the answer to this critical question through a series of false starts and trial and error. Other companies may arrive at the answer by first defining what they mean by *normal* business operations; identifying the level of business interruption the company can sustain before its survival is threatened; and identifying what "recovery" should look like for the organization. *Recovery*, as used herein, can be defined as the ability to operate well enough to meet current obligations to one's network touchpoints at a level that is acceptable to those touchpoints (clients, suppliers, vendors, business partners, your organization), and to protect the life/safety of employees while assuring that strategy and competitive intelligence initiatives are addressed.

The ability to effectively respond to and manage event consequences in a timely manner is essential to ensure your organization's survivability in today's fast-paced business environment. With the emergence of "new threats"—including cyber-terrorism and bio-terrorism—and the increasing exposure of organizations to traditional threats such as fraud, systems failure, fire, product recalls, explosions, spills, natural disasters, etc., the integrated approach to business continuity, as presented herein—based on the concept of graceful degradation and agile restoration—is your best answer.

Chapter One

ENTERING THE AGE OF UNCERTAINTY: WHAT TO EXPECT

Chapter Summary

This introductory chapter provides an overview of the potential situations businesses may face in this time of uncertainty. In this chapter, we will begin our investigation into the development of an effective and, as may be possible, comprehensive business continuity process. We will also discuss the basis for developing vertically and horizontally integrated business continuity systems.

This chapter is designed to provide the reader with sufficient background material to allow you to focus your efforts when developing your organization's "integrated" business continuity process. This and the subsequent chapters in this book build on my two previous books. The first book, entitled *It Can't Happen Here: All Hazards Crisis Management Planning*, published by PennWell in 1993, provides the conceptual background for an approach to the development of an effective "all hazards" event man-

DEFINITION OF TERMS USED IN THIS CHAPTER

Threat
Expression of intent

Hazard
Chance of being harmed

Risk
Probability of occurrence

Vulnerability
Weakness realized

Contingency
Expected action(s)

Consequence
Unexpected results

Business Continuity
Strategy, competitive intelligence, event management

agement plan. My second book, entitled *The Emergency Management Planning Handbook*, published by McGraw-Hill in 1995, took the concepts developed in *It Can't Happen Here: All Hazards Crisis Management Planning* and refined and updated them for the 1990s. This manuscript intends to expand on and offer new insights to redefine the business continuity process as we enter an age of uncertainty and understand the "new threat" environment that we face.

This book is not intended to be a step-by-step cookbook of fill-in-the-blank examples. Rather, the issues presented and the concepts discussed are designed to engage and stimulate the reader with thought-provoking discussion and examples of the redefined business continuity process. Many of the concepts presented can be readily applied to your current organizational setting. Others will have to be modified and reshaped to fit your unique situation.

Threat. A threat is an expression of intent. If I say to you that I am going to kill you, you can legitimately say you have received a threat. We assess and prioritize threats all the time. Threats are for the most part things that we should be cognizant of, not fearful of. Threats are indicators, and indicators are valuable in the assessment phase of business continuity system development.

Hazard. A hazard is the chance of being harmed. An example of a typical hazard would be the common chemical products you might find in your own home.

Risk. A risk is the probability of occurrence. Each time you get into your car or get out of bed, you are risking that something may occur to you.

Vulnerability. A vulnerability is a weakness realized.

Contingency. A contingency is an expected action(s).

Consequence. A consequence is an unexpected result(s).

Business continuity. All initiatives taken to assure the survival, growth, and resilience of the enterprise.

Introduction

Before we can discuss in detail the elements of the "integrated" business continuity process, it's useful to summarize the basic assumptions on which this book has been written. These basic assumptions serve to form the foundation for the framework of the "integrated" business continuity process and this redefinition of business continuity.

Assumption 1:
Businesses are Complex Systems
Operating within Multiple Networks

As depicted in Figure 1-1, modern businesses are complex systems with many touchpoints. Complex business systems, however, generally can be grouped into five essential elements of analysis (EEA):

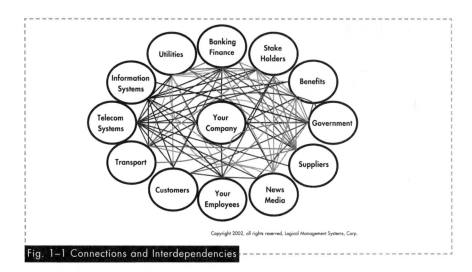

Copyright 2002, all rights reserved, Logical Management Systems, Corp.

Fig. 1–1 Connections and Interdependencies

- Human resources
- Information resources
- Operational resources
- Equipment resources
- Facilities resources

Each of these EEA can be further subdivided into subunits providing measures of effectiveness (MOE) that will enable detailed analysis and assessment. MOEs can be further subdivided into measures of performance (MOP) consisting of specific data points that provide the interrogatives for analysis and assessment. Individual MOPs, with their corresponding data inputs, form the raw data elements that we select for assessment and analysis.

In my consulting practice I have developed the EEA, MOE, and MOP structure into an analysis program I call AUDITRAK[tm]. The AUDITRAK[tm] program currently consists of nine EEA that focus on the assessment of event management elements. As of this writing, modules are under development for the areas of strategy and competitive intelligence.

Assumption 2:
There Are Many Layers of Complexity

Today's complex business system can be viewed as being layered, wherein the outer layer is full functionality and the inner core is minimal stable functionality.

Assumption 3:
Due to Complexity, Analysis of Event Consequences Is Critical

All of a business system's touchpoints within a given network must be considered in order to effectively evaluate vulnerabilities, threats, risks, hazards, and determine the effects of degradation on the business system and therefore the consequences rendered to the business network.

Assumption 4:
Actions Need to Be Coordinated

Each company's actions within the business network will be inadequate unless the entire business network responds in kind.

Assumption 5:
Resources and Skill Sets
Are Key Issues

Today, most companies lack the resources and specialized skills to know what to do to maximize positive business network effects. Figure 1-2 is a depiction of the above assumptions as they apply to the public sector and to the private sector.

Public Sector:

Complex system operating within multiple networks

All of a system's touchpoints within a given network must be considered to effectively evaluate risks, threats, hazards, and vulnerabilities to determine the effects of degradation on the system

Public sector actions at any given level within the network will be inadequate unless the entire network responds in kind

Most levels of public sector lack the resources and specialized skills to know what to do to maximize positive network effects

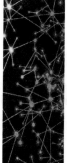

Private Sector:

Complex system operating within multiple networks

All of a system's touchpoints within a given network must be considered to effectively evaluate risks, threats, hazards, and vulnerabilities to determine the effects of degradation on the system

Each company's actions within the network will be inadequate unless the entire network responds in kind

Most companies lack the resources and specialized skills to know what to do to maximize positive network effects

Fig. 1–2 Basic Assumptions

The Facts

As of this writing, the following facts must be considered when developing an integrated business continuity process. They provide a valid assessment of the current environment of uncertainty following the events of Sept. 11, 2001 and subsequent economic events in 2002, such as the Enron and WorldCom bankruptcies and the instances of fraud occurring at Allied Irish Banks and other companies.

- Events that have been building since the end of World War II, including thousands of terrorist attacks on innocent civilians worldwide, have culminated, thus far, in vicious and indiscriminate attacks first by domestic terrorists and now by foreign terrorists on our U.S. homeland

- America is not immune from terrorism. Quite the contrary, we are a target-rich environment for both domestic and international terrorists. The stakes are high, and the issues are indeed life, death, and economic survival

- Terrorists are driven to kill people and to destroy property

- All people and all facilities/operations, and therefore all companies are at risk

- Priority terrorist targets are those of monetary or strategic value, having high human density, and with cultural or symbolic value

- Terrorism is not the only threat to businesses today.

- Corporate headquarters of major corporations present targets of opportunity

- Corporations must take responsibility for their survival. Most of what has to be done in the corporate environment must be done by the corporation. Indeed, it is the corporation's responsibility to its people, stakeholders, and the public relying on its products and services

Government, on the other hand, must concentrate its efforts on ensuring the protection and preservation of "critical infrastructures" essential to the nation's continued well-being. These infrastructures include:

- electric power supplies
- gas and oil
- telecommunications
- banking and finance
- transportation
- water supply systems
- emergency services
- continuity of government services

Corporate America must act immediately to make their key assets (human resources, information resources, equipment, and facilities) unattractive targets. Failure to do so is to be vulnerable to an attack. An integrated approach to business continuity will provide the most effective use of resources; can facilitate risk reduction; and can minimize the potential disruption to the complex network structure of modern business

The Age of Uncertainty

Technology is advancing faster, in many respects, than our capability to harness, manage, and make use of it. Because of its leadership role in this area, the U.S. is the envy of many less technologically advanced nations. We have unrivaled transportation systems, healthcare services, telecommunications, and electrical generation and distribution systems—the list can go on and on. Despite such unparalleled abundance, the gap between "haves" and "have-nots" continues to grow at home. Whatever their station, U.S. citizens have come to expect and demand high reliability in the services we consider essential to our daily lives. When something goes wrong, we get very upset, very quickly.

It is therefore my belief that we live in a world of rapid change and that we have entered into an age of uncertainty. As such, the continuity issue becomes (or should become) one of concern for organizations assuring our daily quality of life. Too many businesses have focused on financial gain to the detriment of their ability to sustain a degradation of service.

After the Sept. 11, 2001 tragedy, I was in New York City for a conference, where I spoke on the need for organizations to develop business continuity systems. I arranged to meet with a colleague who works for a company in New York City. Over dinner, his observations on the fragile state of his organization made me realize the tremendous untold impact of the World Trade Center event. As I listened to him talk, I realized that his organization operated with very thin margins. What's more, it had already begun to delay many programs they had intended to implement due to costs they were incurring in the aftermath of the attack. To go any further in this story would give away the identity of my colleague's business; however, our conversation did enlighten me on several points I need to share here.

One critical point involves the status of the organization's vulnerability, threat, hazard, risk, and consequence-assessment programs: They were incomplete because the organization assumed that vulnerability, threat, hazard, risk, and consequence-assessment are one and the same. These elements *are* intertwined and related; however, they are distinct and different. These programs also mean something entirely different to business than they do to government entities. These elements form the basis for the development of an integrated business continuity system.

It is interesting to note that many business continuity practitioners also use these terms as if they are interchangeable when, in fact, they are not. These concepts need to be treated separately from an assessment and analysis perspective. They also need to be collated and in some instances fused together to determine their relationship and influence on the business continuity process. How this occurs will be discussed in subsequent chapters.

WHAT TO EXPECT

Let's look into my crystal ball and see what's in store for us in the future. Friends have often called me a pessimist because they say I always see the downside to everything. I prefer to consider myself a realist: I look at the future with great expectations and a healthy dose of reality. We live in a world that has seen significant change since the last World War and the end of the Cold War. As the technology transformation continues its ascent at dizzying speeds, the world seems to be less and less capable of managing the acceleration. Fewer and fewer understand the technology. More and more of us are frustrated by the uncertainty of change and the disenfranchisement we feel at work, at home, and in just about every social setting you can name.

We can expect more uncertainty, rapid change, "new threats", and, in general, a potentially rough ride for those who are not prepared. The future will require organizations to be resilient. Ask yourself this question: "Can our organization adjust rapidly to change?" If the answer is "No" or "I am not sure," then you should run, not walk, to develop an integrated business continuity process for your organization and its value chain.

As I write this chapter, I have prepared a short- and long-term threat trend assessment with an accompanying analysis for key segments of the U.S. economy. These have been compiled into Table 1-1. I chose to focus on the U.S. economy primarily because it is the driver of the world economy in many ways.

Segment	Short-Term Trend	Long-Term Trend	Analysis
Commercial real estate	Security demands will remain level or decline as a result of relaxation since the September 11th events	Security demands will increase over time (i.e., suicide bombers, etc.)	Regulations are being initiated (i.e., Chicago) Security issues will be a concern for commercial real estate
Utilities (electric, gas and other infrastructure power supplies)	Near-term security demands will increase due to the perceived threat environment	Security demands over the long term should stabilize as the utility industry addresses high profile targets (fixed facilities) However, transmission systems are susceptible to disruptio n	Utilities, in general, need greater security and business continuity assistance due to the lack infrastructure being replaced The grid system is integrated to the point that a disruption can cascade throughout the system quickly
Energy industry (oil and gas)	Near-term security demands will increase due to the perceived threat environment	Long-term security demands remain high as U.S. dependency on foreign supplies (crude and refined) continues High profile targets (fixed facilities) remain vulnerable Pipeline systems, storage facilities, and other transmission systems (i.e., ship and land transport) continue to be susceptible to disruption	U.S. has reduced its refining capacity by more than 53% leaving the U.S. dependent on foreign sources Dependence on information systems to operate facilities, pipelines, etc. creates security vulnerabilities for this industry
Communications industry (voice, data, and other information systems, etc.)	Security demands will remain level or decline as a result of relaxation since September 11th events	Security demands will increase due to new cyber threats The industry will remain vulnerable to physical disruption to high profile targets (transmission lines, fixed sites, etc.)	Heavy dependence on information systems for operations creates security vulnerabilities for this industry Software code being developed is susceptible to sabotage

Table 1–1 Long- and Short-Term Threat Trend Assessment

Segment	Short-Term Trend	Long-Term Trend	Analysis
Banking and finance	Security demands will remain level or decline as a result of relaxation since September 11th events	Security demands should continue at high levels due to regulatory initiatives and location of high profile targets (fixed facilities) Information systems will continue to be susceptible to disruption	Heavy dependence on information systems for operations creates security vulnerabilities New regulations will require the industry to devote more attention to business continuity and security
Transportation	Security demands will remain high, however, consistency of application will be sporadic	Air, land, and sea transport will see increased demand for a broad range of security services Cargo security will be a high profile area Port, distribution, and staging areas will receive heightened scrutiny due to the high potential for an event at these touchpoints	Difficult to ensure security enforcement, information systems are vulnerable Human resource issues will be an ongoing concern More attention must be paid to staff training, background investigation requirements, staff retention, service quality, and ability to respond to and manage events
Water supply systems	Security demands will be high, however, supply systems will remain vulnerable	Water systems will remain highly vulnerable due to a lack of security resources	Information systems used for operation create security vulnerabilities
Emergency services	Preparedness demands remain high, focus on response to weapons of mass destruction (WMD)	WMD threat is high; delivery system for WMD is a "wild card" with regard to casualties	Emergency services providers will continue to provide services at a high level. WMD threat poses issues
Continuity of government	Protection of population and infrastructure will remain a key issue	Demands will grow with targeting of government facilities for disruption	Disruption of government is difficult Focus on WMD may provide opportunity for an event to occur in other threat areas

Table 1–1 Continued . . .

I have further organized our look at the future into the following areas. They can be viewed as subsets of the categories cited in the table and may provide more specific insights than the broad generalizations made there:

- Human factors
- Infrastructure
- Capital assets (facilities, equipment, etc.)
- Intangible assets (knowledge, intelligence, information network)
- Value chain (domestic, foreign)
- Technology

Human factors. This is the "wild card" category, as I see it. Human factors present one of the most unpredictable areas for the future. How will humans react to the events unfolding even as this book is being written? Companies appearing to be viable suddenly collapsing—taking with them investments and affecting the retirement plans for many. Pressures to survive in the workplace, at home, socially, nationally, and internationally are increasing. With ongoing technological innovation comes the acceleration of everything.

People are less patient, more stressed, and have a greater tendency to act out their frustrations. When they exit the workplace for another job or retirement, they are taking essential skills with them. People entering the workplace lack the skills to replace what is being lost. In many instances, people entering the workplace also have different ethics, morals, and codes of conduct. This will affect how organizations do business. If we look at the complexity assumption, human factors are one of the key components that must be assessed.

Infrastructure. Infrastructure worldwide is going to be put to the test in the near future. In the U.S., our infrastructure systems are already beginning to be stretched to their limits. As corporate America downsizes/right-sizes/reorganizes (and continues the process), we are creating a greater dependency on assuring our standard of living through external sources. The world at large is also faced with infrastructure concerns; most of Europe (including the former Soviet Union) is facing aging infrastructure issues. In the developing nations, infrastructure is a major concern on a daily basis.

Capital assets (facilities, equipment, etc.). After their massive efforts to address the Year 2000 (Y2K) transition, many industries have let their attention lapse, allowing infrastructure issues to not be addressed. Capital assets are often looked at as liabilities instead of assets, and recent events—such as the Enron and Global Crossing debacles—have not changed the focus in this area. Yet, as corporations worldwide continue to focus on the bottom line, capital assets will remain under scrutiny. As a result, fixed assets will remain vulnerable to events like the World Trade Center attack.

Intangible assets (knowledge, intelligence, information network). "Information is power," as the old saying goes. We live in a world that grows smaller and smaller as more and more people gain access to information. Some predict that Chinese will become the dominant language of the Internet in a relatively few years—a prediction deduced, of course, because of the enormous population of that country. We should not overlook India and other parts of Asia in that equation.

Corporations and government are faced with the challenge of assuring the flow of information and securing its protection. (One of the fastest growing crimes is identity theft.) Knowledge management will be a prime focus for business continuity planning in the future.

When we link strategic planning, competitive intelligence, and event management into an integrated business continuity planning process we see that these traditionally distinct areas are interdependent. Every event is a violation of strategy (mission, vision, and values). As such, competitive intelligence initiatives (information management in the form of acquisition and denial) must be reassessed and reshaped. This creates a need for a business continuity system that can assure operational resilience and the survivability of the enterprise.

Value chain (domestic, foreign). Most of the value-added elements in business today are created by knowledge-based service activities such as research and development, marketing research, and customer information. The *value chain*, for the purposes of this book, is defined as all of the touchpoints that your organization encounters as it conducts its primary business functions. Your business continuity initiatives should assess all of these touchpoints as they relate to strategy, competitive intelligence, and event management. All too often, the analysis stops at the boundary of the organization. We can no longer make the assumption that the value chain (upstream = suppliers, partners, vendors, etc.; downstream = customers, resellers, distributors, wholesalers, etc.) is consistent with our mission, vision, and value proposition.

Concluding Thoughts

The development and implementation of a strategic plan charts the course your organization will use to move into and secure its future. Mission, vision, and values are core elements of strategy. Competitive intelligence—the acquisition and/or denial of information—is an integral part of the strategy process. Event management—the ability to identify, react, manage, recover, and adjust effectively to events that threaten to disrupt the operation of the business (*i.e.*, cause strategy to be violated)—combined with strategy and competitive intelligence form the basis for the integrated business continuity processes.

Vision is important to organizational success. Competitive intelligence shapes vision. Disruptive events are prevalent in modern organizations. Every disruptive event your organization experiences is a violation of its strategic vision. Every disruptive event, therefore, demands a modification of strategy and competitive intelligence initiatives. Global competition is now a reality in most sectors, spelling an end to protected domestic markets and safe, reliable profits. Businesses cannot afford to view business continuity as an adjunct; they must view business continuity as a way of doing business. Development and implementation of an integrated business continuity process—from the top down and the bottom up—are essential for businesses to survive, grow, and assure resilience in these uncertain times.

The following chapters introduce the concepts, tools, and process for developing an integrated business continuity process. I hope you will read these chapters with an open mind and see the possibilities for evolving the concepts presented.

References

Davis, Stanley M., Christopher Meyer, *Blur: The Speed of Change in the Connected Economy*, 1998

Mitroff, Ian, I. Avoid "E3" Thinking, *Management General*, 1998

———*Smart Thinking for Crazy Times: The Art of Solving the Right Problems*, 1998

Sikich, Geary W. *It Can't Happen Here: All Hazards Crisis Management Planning*, PennWell Publishing, 1993

———*The Emergency Management Planning Handbook*, McGraw-Hill Books, 1995

———Logical Management Systems, Corp. AUDITRAK^{tm} Diagnostic Assessment Program (www.logicalmanagement.com)

———"Multimedia Strategies for Asset Management: Framework for Emergency Management Planning," *American Institute of Chemical Engineers*, 1994

———"The Financial Side of Crisis," 5th Annual Seminar on Crisis Management and Risk Communication, American Petroleum Institute, 1994

———"Year 2000 Contingency Planning," Institute of Gas Technology, 1999

———"Understanding the Y2K Business Continuity Planning Process," International Quality & Productivity Center, 1999

———"Business Continuity Plans: Crisis Management for a Smooth Transition into the Next Millennium," International Quality & Productivity Center, 1999

———"Managing Crisis at the Speed of Light," *Disaster Recovery Journal* Conference, 1999

———"Strike and Workplace Disruption Planning Guidelines," American Society for Industrial Security, 1999

———Statement for the Congressional Record, 1999; "Chemical Industry Vulnerability: An Overview of Potential Year 2000 Vulnerability Issues & Chemical Industry Preparedness"

———"Business Continuity & Crisis Management in the Internet/E-Business Era," *Teltech*, 2000

———"Are You Prepared for a Disaster?" Physicians Insurers Association, 2000

———"What is there to know about a crisis?" *John Liner Review*, vol. 14, no. 4, Winter 2001

———"Assessing Vulnerabilities and Prioritizing Response," Gas Technology Institute, Emergency Response Conference, May 2001

———"Product Recall: Implications for Business Continuity Planners," *John Liner Review*, vol. 15, no. 2, Summer 2001

———"September 11th Aftermath: Seven Things Your Organization Can Do Now," *Disaster Recovery Journal*, Winter 2002, vol. 15, no. 1

———"The World We Live In: Are You Prepared for Disaster?" Crisis Communication Series, Placeware and ConferZone web-based conference series Part I, January 24, 2002

————"September 11th Aftermath: Ten Things Your Organization Can Do Now," *John Liner Review*, Winter 2002, vol. 15, no. 4

————"Preparing Your Business for a Crisis," Crisis Communication Series, Placeware and ConferZone web-based conference series Part II, February 21, 2002

————"How to Design, Develop and Implement a Successful Drill and Exercise Program," Business Continuity & Contingency Planning Congress, International Quality and Productivity Center, March 17, 2002

————"Business Disasters and Preparing and Internal Communication Plan," Crisis Communication Series, Placeware and ConferZone web-based conference series Part III, March 28, 2002

————"All Hazards," Crisis Management Planning Workshop Logical Management Systems, Corp., 2002

————"Graceful Degradation and Agile Restoration," white paper, Logical Management Systems, Corp., March 2002

————"Graceful Degradation and Agile Restoration Synopsis," *Disaster Resource Guide*, 2002

————"Aftermath September 11th, Can Your Organization Afford to Wait?" New York State Bar Association, Federal and Commercial Litigation, Spring Conference, May 2002

————"September 11th, Can Your Organization Afford to Wait?" GlobalContinuity.com, May 2002

————"Ten Things Your Organization Can Do Now!", The International Emergency Management Society, 9th Annual Conference Proceedings, May 2002

————"How to Design, Develop and Implement a Successful Business Continuity Program", the International Emergency Management Society, 9th Annual Conference Proceedings, May 2002

————"Developing an Effective Crisis Management System for Cargo Security Managers," National Cargo Security Council, Annual Conference, June 2002

————"7 Minutes to Chaos," presentation to the Business Continuity Planners Association of Chicago, July 2002

————"Business Continuity in Times of Uncertainty: Building Pyramids, Cathedrals or Sandcastles," *Disaster Recovery Journal* Fall Conference, September 2002

————"7 Minutes to Chaos: What Federal, State and Local Responders should expect when dealing with the Business Community," National Institute for Government Innovation, Annual Conference, September 2002

United States Government Printing Office, *Report of the President's Commission on Critical Infrastructure Protection*, 1997

Chapter Two

CRITICAL INFRASTRUCTURES: OPPORTUNITIES AND VULNERABILITIES

Chapter Summary

In this chapter, we discuss the vulnerabilities affecting critical infrastructures in the U.S., and what can be done to reduce your enterprise's exposure to disruption should a critical infrastructure become impaired or suffer degradation sufficient to cause a "crisis" within your organization. The critical infrastructures discussed are:

- electric power supplies
- gas and oil
- telecommunications
- banking and finance
- transportation
- water supply systems
- emergency services
- continuity of government

DEFINITION OF TERMS USED IN THIS CHAPTER

Infrastructure
Stand-alone basic structure

Information and communications
Voice, data handling services

Banking and finance
Money handling and
financial services

Physical distribution
Utilities (E, G, W)
transportation (A, L, S)

Energy
Exploration, production,
refining, marketing

Vital human services
Continuity of government,
emergency services

We divide these infrastructures into five "sectors" based on the common characteristics of the included industries. The sectors are:

- information and communications
- banking and finance
- energy (including electric power, oil, and gas)
- physical distribution
- vital human services

The "sectors" are modeled after work performed by the President's Commission on Critical Infrastructure Protection (PCCIP). In 1996, the PCCIP characterized the sectors, studied their vulnerabilities, and sought solutions in the event of disruptions. We will further discuss these vulnerabilities and seek solutions that you can apply to your enterprise's current situation.

This chapter is intended to serve as the basis for your assessment of potential hazards, threats, and vulnerabilities. The outcome you should obtain at the conclusion of this chapter is an appreciation of the potential events that could befall your organization, their effects, and ways to identify and mitigate their consequences.

Infrastructure. An underlying foundation or basic structure supporting economic activity, and national interests or serving a vital purpose for an economy, economic activity, or business.

Information and communications. All voice, data, and information-handling mechanisms, including the hardware and facilities supporting transmission, reception, analysis, and assurance of privacy.

Banking and finance. All money handling, stock, bond, financial risk, insurance mechanisms supporting an economy in the free flow of trade.

Physical distribution. All mechanisms for the distribution of vital power supplies, transportation of goods, and movement of people and products in support of economic activities.

Energy. All fuel sources and related products, their production, refinement, and marketing in support of economic activity.

Vital human services. All support services assuring the safety of the general public and national defense, and rendering aid in support of events that impact an economy, nation, state, or local area.

Introduction

We take for granted the infrastructures on which we depend for our businesses, communities, and country to function effectively and efficiently. Yet, the dramatic events of Sept. 11, 2001 forever changed the way we live; the security of the nation's infrastructure is now a key concern of the White House as well as the boardroom. And while massive modifications to business techniques and systems management brought on by the information revolution cannot be overstated or under-appreciated, traditional businesses modifying their processes to take advantage of the competitive benefits of technology frequently overlook business continuity, security, and "risk" (threat, hazard, and vulnerability) management— not to mention consequence management!

SCENARIOS FOR UNCERTAIN TIMES

Imagine the following scenario. A foreign government, at odds with the U.S. over sanctions imposed on it, targets one of our critical infrastructures—specifically, the petrochemical industry—with the goal of disrupting a critical driver of the U.S. economy. However, there will be no bombs raining down from the sky or explosions caused by saboteurs; there will be devastation of a different kind.

Using a new breed of warrior—the information warrior—the foreign government hacks into the information systems that control the flow of petrochemical products throughout the U.S. Once in, the hackers begin to alter the data and operational codes of systems controlling the flow of raw materials and finished products. They are patient in their nefarious enterprise. For all intents and purposes, systems that control the flow and processes seem to be operating within parameters. Then, one day, without warning, control room operators at refineries, petrochemical facilities, pipelines, and terminals begin to experience a variety of problems—valves do not operate, gauges give false readings, systems begin to shut down for no apparent reason. Soon, confusion turns into panic—panic, into chaos. Tankers cannot unload raw materials. The flow of products in pipelines is disrupted. The flow of raw materials to process units is curtailed.

Emergency plans are activated. Calls are made to activate emergency response teams. There is, however, one small problem that becomes very apparent: The emergency response teams have nothing to do in the way of response. That's because typical emergency response teams are not trained, prepared, or equipped to deal with an *information* systems attack. They are trained, prepared, and equipped to deal with fires, spills, and explosions. However, none of these have occurred—as yet.

Rapidly, all layers of management within the system begin to get involved in the response. "Crisis management" plans are activated, though for the majority of the responding entities, again, these plans offer little assistance, since they have focused, for the most part, on how to address the media during a crisis. The plans will prove valuable only later, when the media begins to report in earnest on the events disrupting America.

Now upper management becomes involved. Questions are raised. Answers are sought. Information systems personnel at all levels are feverishly trying to undo the damage. Successes come in small increments. It takes more than a month to get systems back to 90% of operating capacity—a month that has changed the face of America. The U.S. is in the grip of winter. There are shortages in heating oil, gasoline, and diesel fuel.

The American economy begins to grind to a halt. Prices start to skyrocket. Food shortages occur as the transportation system is impacted. Telecommunications systems are disturbed. Public utilities are upset. Banking and finance centers suffer losses. Share prices of the affected oil company stocks tumble on Wall Street. Soon, a cascading effect causes other stocks to tumble; personal investments and savings are, in some cases, wiped out. Credit card debt soars. Water supply systems, government, and related services are affected.

As businesses begin the recovery process, analysis is undertaken. "How could this have happened?" seems to be a constant question on everyone's lips.

In one month's time the basic foundations of America's vibrant economy are shaken. The effect is like dominos, cascading throughout the world...

Sound like the stuff of science fiction or the latest Jack Higgins, Tom Clancy, or Frederick Forsyth novel? Perhaps; but if we remember back to the fateful hours and days after the events of Sept. 11, 2001 we will also recall that gasoline prices at some stations skyrocketed to more than $5.00 per gallon. While this did not last long, and refunds were made in many cases, we see how quickly panic (and greed) can affect prices. At the time of their initial studies, the PCCIP also saw this as an all-too-real scenario.

If your appetite hasn't been whetted yet, here are some additional examples of what may lie ahead:

Thirsty? Drink up!

Think about this, the next time you turn on the faucet to fill your glass with cold water for a drink. What if a disgruntled worker at a water treatment facility in your city was to pour five gallons of trichloroethylene (TCE) into the treated water heading for your tap? One gallon of TCE will contaminate approximately 292,000,000 gallons of water beyond the safe drinking water standard established by the U.S. Environmental Protection Agency (EPA).

Have a nice commute!

Rush hour on Chicago's Dan Ryan Expressway (or your city, your freeway artery—take your pick). A truck in front of you slows, and you see his hazard lights start to flash. Traffic, which has been at a crawl, comes to an almost dead halt. The man stops the truck in the middle of the freeway, blocking off two lanes and snarling traffic in all four lanes as motorists attempt to negotiate around the stalled vehicle. The truck has impacted all traffic, under an overpass, on one of the busiest freeways in the world. You curse at the driver as he gets out—just another motorist with a problem—and as he lifts the hood; apparently he has had a breakdown. He appears to be working on a problem with the engine, but in reality he is setting the timer on a device that will detonate a bomb. A car stops; its driver appears to be offering assistance. The truck's driver gets in the car. The car drives away, leaving the abandoned truck.

On your way home?

You observe a man in your local train station at rush hour. Neither you, nor anyone else, pay much attention as the man drops a crumpled piece of tin foil that looks like a spent candy wrapper. No one notices the flesh-colored rubber gloves he is wearing. He proceeds through the busy terminal nonchalantly dropping more crumpled up candy wrappers.

People tread over the tin foil, spreading the contents throughout the terminal and onto the trains departing the city. It's not candy wrappers the man has dropped. It happens to be a biological agent, and it's being spread through the air as people trample the tin foil wrappers on their way to their trains and home. By the time you get home, you feel the symptoms of the flu coming on. You go to the bathroom and get some Alka-Seltzer cold tablets and a couple of Tylenol and decide to go to bed early.

Tune in to CNN for more information—that is, if your television is working!

An underground group targets your city's electrical distribution grid, planting bombs at unmanned substations. After a series of explosions, your power goes out. You and many of your neighbors and local businesses are in the dark. Television, telephone, and other services are disrupted. Utility crews frantically attempt to make repairs.

AS A HACKER PENETRATES, WANT TO WRITE THAT CHECK FOR THE MORTGAGE?

A hacker penetrates the firewalls of a major bank and begins to manipulate several accounts—one of which happens to be yours. The hacker also puts a code into the bank's main computer files. He knows that his unauthorized activities will eventually be discovered, but is fairly sure that the apparently innocuous line of code he has inserted will be extremely difficult to discover among the millions of lines of code operating your bank's systems—that is, until it is activated, with devastating consequences.

OR...GO AHEAD; YOU CAN COME UP WITH SOMETHING!

Could we be affected by such events as these in the future?

The PCCIP thought so in 1997. Today, we hear warnings and predictions just as dire from highly respected persons, such as the Secretary of Defense and the director of Homeland Security.

Critical Infrastructures— Critical Vulnerabilities?

Under Executive Order 13010, certain national infrastructures have been identified and designated as being so vital that their incapacity or destruction would have a debilitating impact on the defense or economic security of the U.S.

On October 15, 1997 the President's Commission on Critical Infrastructure Protection (PCCIP) presented its report on critical infrastructure vulnerabilities to President Clinton. The report highlighted a significant dilemma facing the U.S.—one that my research has since confirmed: The growing interdependence of critical infrastructures.

For example, water, sewage, and other public utilities are commonly linked within a city's control system. As technology continues to advance at an accelerated pace, so does the means for those bent on disruption and mayhem, or even less nefarious pursuits, to interdict such an increasingly interdependent system upon which we depend on for our quality of life and economic well-being.

Expectations—we all have them. You turn on the light switch and expect the lights to function. You turn the thermostat up and expect heat; turn it down and expect cool air. You lift the telephone receiver and expect a dial tone. You turn on the tap and expect clean, drinkable water. Ask yourself one question: What if...? What if the lights didn't go on, the heat or cooling didn't work, you picked up the telephone and didn't get a dial tone? The report of the PCCIP states in its introduction:

> *The United States is in the midst of a tremendous cultural change, a change that affects every aspect of our lives. The cyber dimension promotes accelerating reliance on our infrastructures and offers access to them from all over the world, blurring traditional boundaries and jurisdictions. National defense is not just about government anymore, and economic security is not just about business. The critical infrastructures are central to our national defense and our economic power, and we must lay the foundations for their future security on a new form of cooperation between the private sector and the federal government.*

To review, the critical infrastructures that were studied consist of:

- electric power supplies
- gas and oil
- telecommunications
- banking and finance

- transportation
- water supply systems
- emergency services
- continuity of government

The Commission divided its work into five "sectors" based on the common characteristics of the included industries. The sectors, again, are:

- information and communications
- banking and finance
- energy (including electrical power, oil, and gas)
- physical distribution
- vital human services

The Commission characterized the sectors, studied their vulnerabilities, and looked for solutions, preparing comprehensive working papers for each of the five sectors and providing specific recommendations. Other sections of the report contain information on issues that are not sector specific. Among them is a paper on research and development recommendations, which outlines a comprehensive set of topics regarding the long-term needs of infrastructure protection.

A paper on national infrastructures contains the Commission's conclusions and recommendations about the functions and responsibilities for infrastructure assurance, and the creation of jointly-staffed units in the federal government and private sector that represent infrastructure owners and operators. Also included in the report is a paper, entitled "Shared Infrastructures, Shared Threats," which analyzes the vulnerabilities and threats facing the critical infrastructures.

While the report recognized the significance of physical threats, it concluded that government and industry have a significant amount of experience in dealing with them. It was the cyber threat that received most of the report's attention. Cyber issues dominated the analysis because networked information systems present fundamentally new security challenges. The Commission found:

> *The development of the computer and its astonishingly rapid improvements have ushered in the Information Age that affects almost all aspects of American commerce and society. Our security, economy, way of life, and perhaps even survival, are now dependent on the interrelated trio of electrical energy, communications, and computers.*

The Chinese have a saying, "Opportunity is always present in the midst of crisis." Such is it with the Commission's report: It shows that America's critical infrastructures underpin every aspect of our lives and that these infrastructures are extremely vulnerable to old and newly identified threats. We need to recognize that the rules have changed. No longer can we react in the way we have been taught to think. If we do, we will not be able to address the threat(s) effectively.

While a satchel full of dynamite or a truckload of fertilizer and diesel fuel are both recognized threats with known outcomes, the specter of cyber threats is one that hangs over our heads like the sword of Damocles. Today, the right command sent over a network to a power-generating station's control computer could be just as effective as a backpack full of explosives, and the perpetrator would be harder to identify and apprehend. The Commission stated:

> *...rapid growth of a computer-literate population ensures that increasing millions of people possess the skills necessary to consider such an attack. The wide adoption of public protocols for system interconnection and the availability of "hacker tool" libraries make their task easier.*

One must also consider the resources required for conducting a physical attack versus those to conduct a cyber attack. Physical attacks generally dictate a large logistics operation, while the resources for a cyber attack generally consist of a personal computer and a simple telephone connection to an Internet service provider anywhere in the world. Today this is enough to cause a great deal of harm.

The Commission recognized that our energy and communications infrastructures, already growing in complexity and operating closer to designed capacity, present an increased vulnerability with the almost guaranteed possibility of cascading effects on the other infrastructures. Because of their technical complexity, some of these dependencies may be unrecognized until a major failure occurs.

A WIDE SPECTRUM OF THREATS—IS YOUR ORGANIZATION VULNERABLE?

Of the many people with the necessary skills and resources, some may have the motivation to cause substantial disruption in services or destruction of the equipment used to provide the service. The Commission compiled a list of the kinds of threats and the scope of potentially adverse consequences for the infrastructures. They recognize that it may not be possible to categorize the threat until the perpetrator is identified (e.g., we may not be able to distinguish industrial espionage (competitive intelligence initiatives) from national intelligence collection). The report cited the following examples:

Natural events and accidents. Storm-driven wind and water regularly cause service outages, but the effects are well known, the providers are experienced in dealing with these situations, and the effects are limited in time and geography.

Blunders, errors, and omissions. By most accounts, incompetent, inquisitive, or unintentional human actions (or omissions) cause a large fraction of the system incidents that are not explained by natural events and accidents. Since these usually only affect local areas, service is quickly restored; but there is potential for a nationally significant event.

Insiders. Normal operations demand that a large number of people have authorized access to facilities or to associated information and communications systems. If motivated by a perception of unfair treatment by management, or if suborned by an outsider, an "insider" could use authorized access for unauthorized disruptive purposes.

Recreational hackers. For an unknown number of people, gaining unauthorized electronic access to information and communication systems is a most fascinating and challenging game. Often they deliberately arrange for their activities to be noticed even while hiding their specific identities. While their motivations do not include actual disruption of service, the tools and techniques they perfect among their community are available to those with hostile intent.

Criminal activity. Some are interested in personal financial gain through manipulation of financial or credit accounts or stealing services. In contrast to some hackers, these criminals typically hope their activities will never be noticed, much less attributed to them. Organized crime groups may be interested in direct financial gain or in covering their activity in other areas.

Industrial espionage (Competitive Intelligence initiatives). Some firms find or invent reasons to discover the proprietary activities of their competitors—by open means if possible or by criminal means if necessary. Often these are international activities conducted on a global scale.

Terrorism. A variety of groups around the world would like to influence U.S. policy and are willing to use disruptive tactics if they think that will help.

National intelligence. Most, if not all, nations have at least some interest in discovering what would otherwise be secrets of other nations for a variety of economic, political, or military purposes.

Information warfare. Both physical and cyber attacks on our infrastructures could be part of a broad, orchestrated attempt to disrupt a major U.S. military operation or a significant economic activity.

Lack of Awareness = Lack of Preparedness?

Not only is the general public, to a great extent, seemingly unaware of the extent of the vulnerabilities in the services we all take for granted, the Commission found that "within government and among industry decision makers, awareness is limited." Interviews with industry and government decision makers revealed "that there has not yet been a cause for concern sufficient to demand action."

It is not surprising that infrastructures have always been attractive targets for those who would do us harm. In the past we have been protected from hostile attacks on the infrastructures by broad oceans and friendly neighbors. Today, the evolution of cyber threats has changed the situation dramatically. In cyberspace, national borders are no longer relevant. Electrons don't stop to show passports.

PRESIDENT'S COMMISSION ON CRITICAL INFRASTRUCTURE PROTECTION REPORT

The Commission recommended several actions, in its report, that should be considered to increase public and private sector sensitivity to these threats and reduce our vulnerabilities at all levels.

To counter the lack of awareness, a national focus or advocate for infrastructure protection is needed. Following up on their report to the President, the Commission recommended, "We need to build a framework of effective deterrence and prevention." They recognized that,

> *These infrastructures are so varied, and form such a large part of this nation's economic activity, that no one person or organization can be in charge. ... With the existing rules, you may have to solve the crime before you can decide who has the authority to investigate it.*

The threat of an imminent attack or a credible threat sufficient to warrant a sense of immediate national crisis existed prior to and, most assuredly, exists since the events of Sept. 11, 2001. However, very little has been done to take action to reduce our vulnerabilities. We should also note that with globalization by U.S. industries, we have become even more vulnerable to disruption as the result of an external event that has no apparent impact on the U.S., as was seen by financial troubles in Southeast Asia in the late 1990s.

YOUR QUANDARY: WHAT TO DO?

How prepared is your company to deal with the loss of critical infrastructures vital to its survival? A better question might be, "Can your company identify the critical infrastructures upon which it depends for its survival?"

Does your current business continuity plan address the questions discussed thus far? Take some time to complete the following simple analysis in Figure 2-1 and see how your organization fares. The LMSCARVER™ analysis is a tool I have refined and use in my consulting engagements during the initial phase of analysis. It is based on targeting practices utilized by military elements and a combination of business risk assessment methodologies. In order to effectively answer the questions, some definition of terms used in the analysis process will be helpful.

The first element is *criticality*. A determination as to the criticality of the service, product, etc. being supplied via the value chain is essential if you are going to adequately assess the potential risk exposure. Once criticality is established, an assessment of *accessibility* is necessary. By accessibility, I am referring to how accessible an item is.

One needs to assess the accessibility to the item, the accessibility to alternative items that can be substituted, and the accessibility of the item to disruption. Once criticality and accessibility are established, you need to determine *recognizability*, *i.e.*, how readily recognizable is the item with respect to its loss from your organization's value chain? If I am targeting your organization, I am going to look at readily recognizable items that can be accessed and are critical to your operations.

Once the first three items' weighting parameters are established, one must determine the *vulnerability* presented by the potential loss of the element in your value chain. For example, let's say you're a distributor concerned over critical inventory. Your information systems may be able to accurately account for your inventory, but if you were to lose access to your inventory supply location or ability to move the inventory to market, it would not matter how accurately you could determine the level of inventory, as you and your customers would not be able to access the items. Therefore, a *vulnerability* can be defined as the potential for any degradation, interruption, or non-recoverability to such an extent that the consequence is likely to result in harm to the organization, harm to others (suppliers, customers, etc.), and/or substantial negative financial impact.

A vulnerability can arise from:

- false *assumption*
- blocked or altered *component*
- blocked or altered *function*
- blocked or altered *operation*

Once you have established criticality, accessibility, recognizability, and vulnerability, you must determine the *effect* of the loss of the value chain item. Effect can (and will generally) associate to the impact of the loss. However, one must consider all aspects of effect, as there can and may be some positive effect arising from the loss or interdiction of the value chain.

Lastly, one must determine aspects of *recouperability* associated with the potential loss or disruption. That is: How resilient is my organization? Can we quickly respond to, manage, and recover from a disruption of the value chain? The net result of conducting a LMSCARVER™ analysis is to be able to determine the potential significance of an event from a consequence management perspective.

INSTRUCTIONS

Use a separate sheet of paper for each touchpoint listed in the figure in your organization's value chain. On the second part of the questionnaire, rank each touchpoint using the number scale 1–5, where 1 is of lowest importance and 5 is of highest importance. Provide comments as to why you rated the touchpoint as you did. From this top-level assessment, you can begin to get a picture of your organization's network complexity, the touchpoints that are critical, and the infrastructure dependencies for your organization. You can use this assessment to determine the scope of your business continuity plan, the organizational elements required for the planning process (vesting them with ownership), and the external entities with which you should coordinate for planning purposes. You can also use this type of form for vetting vendors, suppliers and other value chain partners.

Note that at the bottom of the form is a box entitled, "Consequence Management Significance." As you complete the forms, give some thought to what the consequences would be if you were unable to access or utilize a touchpoint for a given period of time. What duration increments would you consider as time-critical, time-sensitive, and time-dependent?

This last question is one you and your organization should be very interested in assessing and addressing. Again: What duration increments would you consider as time- critical, time-sensitive, and time-dependent? In order to answer this question, you must be able to define the terms time-critical, time-sensitive, and time-dependent as they apply to your organization. Table 2-1 provides a set of sample parameters that can be used to determine the criteria for definition. Note that, in every circumstance, the broad-based definitions need to be custom-fitted to your particular situation. They may also vary within your organizational structure from level to level, vertically and horizontally across the organization. With this in mind, one should seek input from the organization and not set arbitrary criteria as a definition of terms.

Directions: The LMSCARVER™ analysis form is designed to facilitate the evaluation of risks, threats, hazards, and vulnerabilities for your organization and to determine the consequences of touchpoint degradation to your organization. Choose a touchpoint from part 1 for analysis. Insert the named touchpoint into the area of analysis box in Part 2 and complete the LMSCARVER™ analysis ranking the touchpoint using the numeric rating system. Complete Part 3 by filling the consequence management significance to your organization.

Part 1: Organization TouchPoints

Touchpoint	Touchpoint
Electric power supplies	Operational infrastructure (specify)
Gas and oil systems	Customers
Telecommunications systems	Internal systems
Banking and finance systems	Facilities
Transportation systems	Equipment
Water supply systems	Human resources key personnel
Emergency Services	Human resources staff elements
Continuity of government services	Contract services (specify)
Suppliers	Other (specify)

Part 2: TouchPoint Analysis

Area of Analysis:	Lowest		Highest			Comments
	1	2	3	4	5	
C = Critical						
A = Accessible						
R = Recognizable						
V = Vulnerable						
E = Effect						
R = Recoverable						
Totals						

Part 3: Consequence Management Significance

Fig. 2–1 LMSCARVER™ Analysis Elements

Note that Table 2-1's time frame is stated in days; your circumstances may be such that your organization has a time frame measured differently (in hours, perhaps; in some cases, this time frame is measured in minutes!).

As an example, I offer this situation. I was consulting to a hospital group seeking to determine its needs for a hot site for the data center. We had interviewed the data center personnel and were fairly comfortable with the progress of the assessment. As we began the user group interviews, we were stopped cold in our tracks when the lab group announced that 15 minutes of downtime equated to approximately 4 hours of recovery time for them. After hearing this, we immediately rethought the time-critical, time-sensitive, and time-dependent equations. And this was just an information systems touchpoint vulnerability! The sample is shown in Table 2-1.

Time Critical	Time Sensitive	Time Dependent
0 – 3 Days	4 - 7 Days	8+ Days
Critical infrastructure loss Telecommunications, data, and other information systems Transportation (air, land, water) Utilities (gas, electric, water) Energy supply Critical services Access denial Degradation/loss of critical operations Loss/degradation of operational capability Loss of electrical supply sources Loss of telecommunication data, other information sources Loss/degradation of buildings/occupancy Disruption of transportation Disruption of water supply Disruption of emergency services	Finance Vendor/supplier Business applications Human resources and staffing Legal Oversight/documentation Transition to recovery Organization Recovery operations Humanitarian assistance Infrastructure restoration Information and operations Recovery and synchronization Resumption of critical business functions Full function restoration Permanent restoration	Government relations Corporate relations Corporate image Banking and finance Assigned relocation sites Communication systems requirements Operations systems requirements Personnel requirements Documentation of facilities recovery Assessment of operations requirements Building documents/records required in an emergency Public sector contacts Forms and supplies Associated plans and information Insurance and risk management plan Treasury contingency cash plan Controller's system for tracking recovery expenses Vendor/supplier/ consultant list Floor space alternatives outside main office Records planning, storage and retrieval

Table 2–1 Time-Critical, Time-Sensitive, and Time-Dependent Equations

If I have attempted to cover a lot of ground concerning the important considerations that I feel must be taken into consideration when assessing the consequences of an event, remember that this chapter addresses *critical infrastructures*: I feel it is important to recognize just how interdependent our infrastructure system is! When we take into consideration internal infrastructures and the internal systems they support, we begin to have an appreciation for the complexity of the analysis process. We should also have an appreciation for the need to properly plan for an infrastructure disruption.

I concluded chapter 1 with a look into my crystal ball. Based on the information in the table presented in that chapter, we can further detail the infrastructure considerations expressed. I think it is important to understand how heavily modern organizations rely on the uninterrupted operation of critical infrastructures and the extreme vulnerability of these systems. Neither should one overlook the simple fact that many of the world's infrastructure systems are reaching the limits of their capacity to provide the expected service. They are also being subjected to demands that are taxing the maximum capacity of aging systems. Should demand outstrip the capacity and/or an event occur with the result of severely degrading an infrastructure, the consequences could be felt throughout the world. With this in mind, we need to add an analysis of the *cascading effect* to the assessment paradigm.

External Infrastructure Loss	Cascade Effect
Electrical supply	
Financial services	
Government services	
Voice, data, other information systems	
Transportation (air, land, sea)	
Water supply	
Gas supply	
Internal Infrastructure Loss	**Cascade Effect**
Human resources	
Financial services	
Facilities	
Information services	
Other (list)	
Business Disruption	**Cascade Effect**
Disruption of customer care service	
Communication to/from workforce	
System integrity: safety, reliability	
Availability of critical personnel	
Critical applications integrity issues	
Unauthorized access	
Security compromise	
Operating revenue issues	
Balance sheet issues	
Benefits issues	

Table 2–2 Consequence Management—Cascade Effect

As an example, Table 2-2 is a worksheet you can use to begin to determine the cascading effects of an event that disrupts infrastructure capacity.

As I prepared this table, I realized that one could not include every possible example of a business disruption and the cascading effect that may occur. With that in mind, you can begin to use this framework to custom fit the assessment to your organization's unique circumstances.

Table 2-3 is an example of the possible activities that an organization may undertake in response to an event. Again, this is an example and should be viewed in that context.

Phases of Event Response	Typical Activities
Event reported	Event notification and initial response. Activation of command center issue log tracking system
Assessment/recommendation	Event is assessed (actual damages, impacts), level of severity is determined, recommended actions for mitigating event are developed by the affected entity Event tracked by command center
Workaround	Initiate consequence management plan(s) as appropriate Document workaround steps to be accomplished Event tracked by command center
Resolution/In-process activities	Restoration of affected operations, processes, equipment, facilities, services, etc. In-process activities, periodic updates, sustained response to event Full function restoration of affected processes Event resolution documented Event tracked by command center

Table 2-3 Phases of Event Response and Typical Activities

Critical Infrastructures Assessment

The following provides a brief summary of the PCCIP critical infrastructure vulnerabilities. I highly recommend that readers access the National Infrastructure Protection Center website at http://www.nipc.gov for further information on infrastructure vulnerability, vulnerability updates, and other useful information that can assist you in your planning efforts.

ENERGY INFRASTRUCTURE

We are heavily dependent on the energy infrastructure for the quality of life in modern society. The energy infrastructure includes oil, gas, electric power, natural gas, and the mechanisms supporting the exploration, production, refining, and marketing of energy. This includes all production, processing, and transportation-associated operations. As you can surmise, this infrastructure is one that is vertically and horizontally very expansive. Each element within the infrastructure requires large, complex transportation networks to deliver energy to end-users. Each has transmission and distribution lines. Electric power requires substations and transformers. Oil and gas require pumping stations, refineries, and pipelines. Natural gas requires compressors, gate stations, and processing centers. Storage is also a key component within this infrastructure (except for electricity).

In addition to the physical components that comprise these networks, each element uses sophisticated supervisory control and data acquisition (SCADA) systems. The SCADA systems monitor and operate the complex networks that move the energy supply around in an efficient and safe manner. Each element is dependent on the others and on the telecommunications, data, and information processing systems that are used to operate each.

Degradation or failure of one of these elements tends to have a cascading effect throughout this infrastructure and related infrastructures. One can cite many examples of how important the energy infrastructure is to our daily lives. Some of the emerging threats and issues we face include the following:

- Within the U.S., refining capacity has been reduced by more than 53% while consumption of energy is on the rise

- No new construction in the refining industry has taken place since the late 1960s, early 1970s

- The electric utility grid is going to be affected negatively by the decommissioning of nuclear power plants that are reaching the end of their life cycles. This is also the case with many old fossil fuel plants

- Deregulation and rapid restructuring are occurring throughout this infrastructure

- Competition is reducing operating margins, and this can have a negative effect if the infrastructure experiences disruption, even on a small scale

- Restructuring of the marketplace is changing the way commodities are purchased, sold, and distributed

- Reduced investments in new technology create the potential for less reliable operation and additional disruptions in supply

- Aging infrastructure components present potential concerns because long lead times for construction, licensing, environmental, and other issues must be taken into consideration
- Downsizing, reorganization, and changes in the focus of the energy industry create potential situations for disgruntled personnel to commit acts of sabotage
- As the workforce ages and retires, there is a loss of expertise, experience, and knowledge that is not easily replaced
- Increased dependence on information systems with open architectures, centralized operations, increased communications over public networks, and less maintenance creates significant vulnerabilities
- Dependence in the U.S. on foreign supplies raises concern about reliability of supply
- Worldwide energy demand is increasing
- Technological failure or failure due to cyber attacks presents a greater vulnerability as dependence on automated systems continues to grow

Threats to the U.S. energy infrastructure come from many sources—hostile foreign governments, terrorist groups (domestic and international), disgruntled employees, malicious intruders, natural disasters, accidents, system complexities, and dependence on other infrastructures. Additional challenges facing this infrastructure are many and include vulnerabilities such as—

- operating system changes due to accelerated technologies, network centralization, systems complexities, and open architectures
- potential bypassing of SCADA systems using common hardware and software that connect to company networks and rely on dial-back modems
- increased availability of vulnerability information
- rapid assimilation of advanced technologies with inherent complexities
- consolidation of infrastructure corridors
- system complexity such that a failure has the potential to cascade rapidly throughout the infrastructure and affect other infrastructures

At this writing, we have gone through an energy crisis in California, Enron has collapsed, and other companies have or are experiencing weakness in their operating positions. Companies like Consolidated Edison of New York, strapped by unexpected costs (response to the World Trade Center), are finding their ability to accomplish scheduled tasks (maintenance, etc.) stretched to their limits.

Dependence on foreign refined products puts the U.S. at significant risk. As cited earlier, we saw in the aftermath of the September 11th events gasoline prices rise—in some instances to more than $5.00 per gallon. What would your organization do if we were faced with a sustained energy crisis?

INFORMATION COMMUNICATIONS INFRASTRUCTURE

The three key components of this infrastructure are the physical means for moving data, a network and transportation component, and computing systems. The physical component consists of satellites, optical fibers, copper lines, wireless transmission means, and other "hardware" that support the infrastructure. The network component consists of switching mechanisms and software control systems, dealing with the addressing, routing, and transportation of data. The final component, computing systems, generate, manipulate, store, display, and control information.

This combination provides communication, computation, control, information, and human collaborative systems that are critical to the proper functioning of this and other infrastructures. We are becoming so heavily dependent on this infrastructure that, in many instances, companies are finding once a conversion is made, very little time elapses before it becomes impossible to return to a manual or less automated operation.

This infrastructure also provides the backbone for the Internet and connects with computer and communications networks internationally. The explosive growth of the Internet and continuing leaps in technology, combined with the acceptance of eBusiness and eCommerce by businesses worldwide, open a Pandora's box of threats and vulnerabilities. The advent of the Internet and e-mail systems has brought a new meaning to words like "virus." As a result of more connectivity, we are faced with an increasing need to assure that we are protected. Security in this infrastructure has taken on a new meaning as threats can be actualized from far away locations with the ease of a keystroke.

Threats to the information and communication infrastructure can come from many sources. Deliberate attacks from external and internal sources can include cyber and physical means. Interconnected networks are vulnerable due to lack of protocols, poorly developed protection (firewalls, etc.), and difficulty in identifying the perpetrator of the event. Some of the emerging threats and vulnerabilities to this infrastructure include:

- rapid introduction of new technologies and new features
- ill-defined testing protocols
- system overload
- growing dependence on foreign sources for software coding and development
- data manipulation or destruction

- data storage integrity
- difficult or impossible to de-automate once automation has occurred
- vulnerability detection analysis not well developed
- value today resides in information and relationships; it cannot be seen and often it cannot be measured
- time, space, and mass are being blurred by speed, connectivity, and intangibles
- telecommunications networks in the U.S. carry more electronic data than voice

Boundaries are blurring as everyone becomes electronically connected. Traditional rules governing the conduct of government and business are blurred as businesses are redefined, products become services, services become products, and business lines change constantly. As this change accelerates, it gets more and more difficult for traditional strategists to achieve an accurate focus on the current situation.

BANKING AND FINANCE

The banking and finance infrastructure consists of institutions, agencies, and support systems that facilitate lending, borrowing, issuing, trading in, or caring for money, credit, and other representations of value. Included in this infrastructure are banks, credit unions, insurance companies, lending and credit institutions of all kinds, securities and commodities dealers, state, federal, and international oversight and regulatory bodies, and the web of voice, data, and other communications mechanisms, equipment, and linkages supporting transactions among those systems.

Several emerging trends threaten the safety and soundness of the banking and finance infrastructure:

- Deregulation and increased competition that can result in degradation of the capability to address added security measures
- Convergence of technology in computing, communications, networking, and encryption that increase the efficiency and flexibility of transaction support, but can add vulnerabilities
- Internationalization of commerce, giving new, non-domestic entities unprecedented access to U.S. systems and information
- Changing definitions of value, e.g., the form of money and the way that information about money is managed have become valuable assets

Four challenges face the banking and finance infrastructure:

- Making policy tradeoffs to balance competing goals among open markets, regulatory management, national security, and free trade
- Adapting to the technical revolution on two infrastructures—information and communications, and banking and finance
- Accommodating the internationalization of commerce and information
- Defining new assets requiring protection

Potential threats and vulnerabilities in this infrastructure originate from the lack of a clear understanding of how alternative responses in each of the four areas might affect the infrastructure. According to the authors of the book, *Blur*, financial institutions transferred money at the rate of more than *$41 billion* a minute when the book was written—and this is growing daily. Connectivity, speed, and intangible values are the new driving force in business.

TRANSPORTATION

The transportation infrastructure consists of all surface, air, and waterborne means to move goods. (The PCCIP excluded pipeline systems because they were considered under the energy infrastructure.) When we look at the transportation infrastructure, we see another infrastructure that is complex and has dependencies to other infrastructures. The PCCIP study has subdivided this infrastructure into the following components:

- Public and private airborne and ground-side aviation activity
- Railway and highway movement and transshipment of goods and people
- Inland waterborne commerce and maritime navigation and associated port and terminal activities

When we think of the transportation infrastructure, we must recognize the significance of the two oceans separating the U.S. mainland from Europe and Asia. Since the events of September 11th, concern about port and cargo security has grown.

This infrastructure has seen a decline in the number of entities that comprise it. In addition to seeing the infrastructure (private portion) being held in fewer hands, the Intermodal Surface Transportation Efficiency Act of 1991 has failed to bring about sought-after improvements to the primary and secondary highway system. The desire to reduce costs and increase efficiencies has led to an increasing dependency on information systems and information management technologies as substitutes for capital investment.

Many threats and vulnerabilities exist in the transportation infrastructure. These include:

- cargo security issues
- air transport, airline, and airport security
- passenger, baggage, and cargo handling mechanisms
- port of entry security, port of departure security
- data manipulation and fraud
- cost of replacement, improvement, and/or maintenance for the infrastructure

Recent events have shown how vulnerable the transportation infrastructure is to interdiction by terrorists. Events prior to September 11th, such as the Tokyo subway Sarin gas attacks, also point out the vulnerability of the transportation infrastructure.

The transportation infrastructure is a large part of the U.S. domestic gross national product (GNP), accounting for approximately 16% of GNP. Challenges to the transportation infrastructure center around issues associated with threat identification, reduction of vulnerabilities, and elimination of hazards. These include:

- basic security assurances for passengers and cargo
- fixed and mobile security mechanisms (barriers, alarms, lighting, communication)
- personnel identification and control
- adequate staffing of airport, terminal, port facilities
- information management systems for reporting and decision making
- surveillance of in-transit cargo (goods and people)

VITAL HUMAN SERVICES

The vital human services infrastructure consists of the water supply system, all emergency services (police, fire, rescue, etc.), and continuity of government. The water supply system includes all sources of water—reservoirs, holding facilities, aqueducts, and other transportation means; treatment and filtration systems, distribution systems, delivery systems, cooling systems, and water management systems (runoff control, wastewater, fire-fighting needs, etc.).

The emergency services component performs fire, law enforcement, rescue, and related services on a daily basis. As was evidenced in New York City and at the Pentagon on Sept. 11th, 2001, the emergency services component, though severely tasked, was able to respond and manage.

The continuity of government service component consists of federal, state, and local entities and their ability to provide essential services to the public. One of the lessons learned from September 11th was that the New York City legal system was severely strained by the event. This was due to the closure of the courts. Caseloads (crime did not take a holiday) continued to grow and almost overwhelmed the court system. In addition, the loss of revenue from fines, etc. added to New York City's financial woes. Threats and vulnerabilities within this infrastructure consist of:

- contamination of water supplies from chemical, biological, or other toxic agents
- physical attacks on water supply mechanisms
- cyber attacks on water supply control and management systems
- emergency services (first responders) exposure to chemical, biological, toxic agents, etc.
- inadequate preparation of healthcare providers to deal with mass casualty events
- weapons of mass destruction event overloading healthcare system
- lack of adequate equipment and training for emergency services providers
- dependency of government entities on other infrastructures
- lack of training and adequate civil defense systems in communities throughout the U.S.

Since September 11th, we have seen the creation of the office for Homeland Defense and other initiatives. In January 2002, I wrote two versions of an article entitled, "September 11th Aftermath: Things Your Organization Can Do Now." In the first, I outlined what I thought to be the seven critical things that organizations could do in the post-September 11th time frame. In the second version, I expanded the seven action items to include three additional action items. Table 2-4 highlights the 10 action items that these two articles discussed.

Action #1	Make your enterprise an unattractive target
Action #2	Revise employee screening processes
Action #3	Validate business, community, and government contacts
Action #4	Assess business continuity plans
Action #5	Train and educate your workforce
Action #6	Equip your workforce
Action #7	Review leases and contracts for risk exposure
Action #8	Assess value-chain exposure to supply disruptions
Action #9	Review insurance policies and conduct cost/benefit analysis
Action #10	Communicate commitment

Table 2–4 10 Things Your Organization Can Do Now

On March 11, 2002, I was in New York City for business meetings. A colleague showed me a copy of that day's *Wall Street Journal*, indicating a section entitled, "Workplace Security." In this section was an article "Business's New Agenda." In this article, two tables (Tables 2-5 and 2-6) cited "heightened concerns" and "greater precautions."

Heightened Concerns...	
Topic	**%**
Mail processing	86
Travel	85
Protection of employees	79
Protection of infrastructure	75
Risk assessment	71
Protection of offices and physical plants	69
Employee morale	69
Supply-chain distribution	51
Customer security	50
Productivity	47
Globalization strategies	27
Mergers and strategic alliances	15
Source: Booz Allen Hamilton	

Table 2–5 Heightened Concerns

At the time of this writing, there seems to be a paralysis within the business community, a hesitation to move forward to address the earlier cited issues. Is it that government and business are waiting until the "next shoe" drops before moving forward? In the *Wall Street Journal* article mentioned above, Robert Littlejohn, vice president of global security at Avon Products, Inc. says, "When it is over, people relax, and relaxation brings new vulnerabilities." While I readily agree with the statement, I also feel that relaxation can enable us to *recognize* vulnerabilities.

In the aftermath of the September 11th terrorist attack, we have begun to see America relax. We are in Afghanistan; we are apparently decimating the Al-Qaida and Taliban on a daily basis. Media coverage of the operations has begun to relegate the operations away from the front page of the daily newspaper and away from the top story on the nightly news broadcasts. However, it seems to me that we, as a country and as a people, are not yet ready to come to grips with the fact that the actions being taken against terrorism are just the beginning and will not end with the eradication of the Al-Qaida or Taliban. We are beginning to relax.

...and Greater Precautions	
Topic	**%**
Reviewing disaster-planning document	90
Reviewing insurance policies for adequate coverage	74
Reviewing travel policies	64
Increasing use of videoconferencing	60
Checking backgrounds on contract personnel	51
Checking employee backgrounds more thoroughly	39
Reviewing guidelines for number of staff on any single flight	36
Contracting for emergency alternative office space	35
Increasing use of private or corporate planes	22
Lowering own public profile	7
Source: Booz Allen Hamilton	

Table 2–6 . . . and Greater Precautions

My question to corporate America is this: "Can you afford to relax?" The remainder of this chapter focuses on the need for corporate America to continue to take action to address business survivability in the broadest context.

Executive Order 13224

Today's action disrupts Al-Qaida's communications, blocks an important source of funds, obtains valuable information, and sends a clear message to global financial institutions: You are with us, or with the terrorists. And if you are with the terrorists, you will face the consequences.

President George W. Bush
Nov. 7, 2001
www.whitehouse.gov/news/releases/2001/11/20011107-6.html

Executive Order 13224 signed by President Bush on Sept. 23, 2001 blocks the assets of organizations and individuals linked to terrorism. According to a summary printed in *Counterterrorism & Security Reports, vol. 9, no. 5,* 168, such groups, entities, and individuals are covered by the Executive Order. A complete summary of the executive order (Executive Order 13224 - Blocking Property and Prohibiting Transactions With Persons Who Commit, Threaten to Commit, or Support Terrorism) can be found at www.ustreas.gov/terrorism.

While a complete listing of the organizations covered by the Executive Order is beyond the scope of this book, you can go to www.state.gov/s/ct/rls/fs/2001/6531.htm and find a complete listing.

Executive Order 13224 is important, both because of what it identifies and says, and because of what it does *not* identify and/or say.

While Executive Order 13224 lists some 168 groups, entities, and individuals, it does not list any domestic (U.S.) groups, entities, or individuals bent on committing terrorist acts. I found an interesting website as I researched this: www.tolerance.org provides a map of the U.S. depicting 676 "hate groups" not covered under this Executive Order. One only has to look at the anthrax events and wonder, why not?

In the U.S. and throughout the world, critical infrastructures upon which we all depend for the quality of life we enjoy are at risk. While business leaders express their concerns and list their most compelling topics (Table 2-2), the further away from September 11th that we get without another event, the more relaxed we may become.

Concluding Thoughts

Identification and protection of critical infrastructures will become increasingly important to organizations as they develop their business continuity strategy. Business continuity planning, in the traditional sense, is outdated before it can be implemented. In the next chapter, I offer a suggestion for a new definition of business continuity. However, in closing this chapter, we cannot overlook the importance of the infrastructures that an organization depends on for its existence.

The U.S. is in the midst of a tremendous cultural change—a change that affects every aspect of our lives. The accelerating reliance of our infrastructures on information systems and the cyber dimension is blurring traditional boundaries and jurisdictions. Critical infrastructures are central to any organization's survival. We must lay the foundations for identifying our infrastructure touchpoints and understanding our infrastructure dependencies as we shape business continuity thought.

A paper, "National Structures," contains the conclusions and recommendations of the President's Commission on Critical Infrastructure Protection about the functions and responsibilities for infrastructure assurance. Another useful paper, "Shared Infrastructures: Shared Threats," which summarizes the collected analysis of the vulnerabilities and threats facing the critical infrastructures, added a very useful perspective to my research for this chapter.

The development of the computer and its astonishingly rapid improvements have ushered in an information age that affects almost all aspects of world commerce and society. This has led to dependence on the interrelated trio of electrical energy, communications, and computers. This interconnectedness and interdependency have led to increasing vulnerabilities and threats:

- classical physical disruptions
- cyber threats
- system complexities and interdependencies
- natural events and accidents
- accidental physical damage
- blunders, errors, and omissions
- disgruntled insiders
- recreational hackers
- criminal activity
- industrial espionage
- terrorism
- national intelligence
- information warfare
- lack of awareness
- no national focus

Protection of critical infrastructures will not be accomplished by large government-sponsored projects. It will require continuous attention and incremental improvement for the foreseeable future by everyone. Infrastructures are always going to be attractive targets. As part of your business continuity strategy, you should assure yourself that you have an ongoing program for assessment of critical infrastructures.

References

Bush, George, W., President's Statement to the Nation, November 7, 2001

Davis, Stanley M., Christopher Meyer, *Blur: the Speed of Change in the Connected Society*, 1998

Executive Order 13224 - Blocking Property and Prohibiting Transactions With Persons Who Commit, Threaten To Commit, Or Support Terrorism can be found at www.ustreas.gov/terrorism

National Infrastructure Protection Center, National Structures (www.nipc.gov)

——Shared Infrastructures Shared Threats (www.nipc.gov).

Sikich, Geary W. Logical Management Systems, Corp. (www.logicalmanagement.com), LMSCARVER™ Touchpoint Analysis Diagnostic Program, 2000

——It Can't Happen Here: All Hazards Crisis Management Planning, PennWell Publishing, 1993

——The Emergency Management Planning Handbook, McGraw-Hill Books, 1995

——Managing Crisis at the Speed of Light, Disaster Recovery Journal Conference, 1999

——What is there to know about a crisis, John Liner Review, vol. 14, no. 4, Winter 2001

——Assessing Vulnerabilities and Prioritizing Response, Gas Technology Institute, Emergency Response Conference, May 2001

——September 11th Aftermath: Seven Things Your Organization Can Do Now, Disaster Recovery Journal, Winter 2002, vol. 15, no. 1

——September 11th Aftermath: Ten Things Your Organization Can Do Now, John Liner Review, Winter 2002, vol. 15, no. 4

——"Aftermath September 11th, Can Your Organization Afford to Wait," New York State Bar Association, Federal and Commercial Litigation, Spring Conference, May 2002

——"September 11th, Can Your Organization Afford to Wait?" GlobalContinuity.com, May 2002

——"Ten Things Your Organization Can do Now!" The International Emergency Management Society, 9th Annual Conference Proceedings, May 2002

——Developing an Effective Crisis Management System for Cargo Security Managers, National Cargo Security Council, Annual Conference, June 2002

——7 Minutes to Chaos, Business Continuity Planners Association, July 2002

——Business Continuity in Times of Uncertainty: Building Pyramids, Cathedrals or Sandcastles, Disaster Recovery Journal Fall Conference, September 2002

——7 Minutes to Chaos: What Federal, State and Local Responders should expect when dealing with the Business Community, National Institute for Government Innovation, Annual Conference, September 2002

Tolerance, Hate Groups in the United States, (www.tolerance.org)

United States Government Printing Office, Report of the President's Commission on Critical Infrastructure Protection, 1997

Wall Street Journal, Business's New Agenda, March 11, 2002

Chapter Three

THE UNDERPINNINGS OF BUSINESS CONTINUITY

Chapter Summary

In this chapter, we discuss the relationship between your organization's strategy (its mission, vision, and values), the field of competitive intelligence, and event management.

These three key areas form the basis for redefining business continuity. Today, most value-added business is created by knowledge-based service activities such as research and development, marketing research, and customer information, to cite a few. The development and implementation of a strategic plan chart the course your organization will use to move into the future. Mission, vision, and values are reflective of strategy. Competitive intelligence—the acquisition and/or denial of information—is an integral part of the strategy process. Event management—your business' response, management, and recovery from disruption, and effectively adjusting strategy and competitive intelligence initiatives—is also an integral part of how business should be conducted.

Definition of Terms Used in This Chapter

Strategy
Mission, vision, values

Competitive intelligence
Acquisition, denial operations

Event management
Response, management, recovery operations

Business continuity
Strategy, competitive intelligence, event management

Knowledge management
Institutional repository of understanding

Vision is important to organizational success. Competitive intelligence shapes vision. Disruptive events are prevalent in modern organizations. Every disruptive event your organization experiences is a violation of strategic vision. Every disruptive event, therefore, demands a modification of strategy and competitive intelligence initiatives. Global competition is now a reality in most sectors, spelling an end to protected domestic markets and safe, reliable profits.

Included in this chapter are examples of business continuity strategies, competitive intelligence cycle activities, and event management plans. Topics will include:

- analysis—steps for effective business continuity
- elements of the *integrated* business continuity process
- competitive intelligence business impacts during a disruptive event
- communicating sensitive information
- issues analysis—critical factors facing business today

This chapter is intended to build upon your assessment of potential risks, hazards, threats, vulnerabilities, and their consequences. The outcome you should arrive at is a concept for the structure and application of your business continuity process throughout the various levels of your organization.

Strategy. Underlying principles and foundations that provide focus for the business. Strategy consists of mission, vision, and value statements, and the policies and procedures that support the organization.

Competitive intelligence. All initiatives to assure the acquisition and/or denial of data, information, and other considerations to gain and retain competitive advantage.

Event management. Identification, response, management, monitoring, and recovery initiatives designed to assure the ability of the enterprise to survive.

Business continuity. The combination of strategy, competitive intelligence, event management, and institutional knowledge that assures survivability, growth, resilience, and organizational viability.

Knowledge management. The identification and management of institutional awareness, expertise, skills, and wisdom to support the enterprise.

Introduction

Most value-added business today is created by knowledge-based service activities, such as research and development, marketing research, and customer information, to cite a few. The development and implementation of a strategic plan chart the course your organization will use to move into the future. Mission, vision, and values are reflective of strategy. Competitive intelligence—the acquisition and/or denial of information—is an integral part of the strategy process. Event management—the ability to deal effectively with the consequences of incidents that threaten the effective and efficient operation of your business—is an integral part of business continuity strategy.

Vision is important to organizational success. Competitive intelligence shapes vision. Disruptive events are prevalent in modern organizations. In other words, events occur having unforeseen consequences. Every disruptive event your organization experiences is a violation of its strategy. Every disruptive event, therefore, demands a modification of strategy and competitive intelligence initiatives. As a result of global competition, a disruptive event occurring in a far away place that seemingly has no relation to your business can have near real-time effects on your organization.

Strategy, in the traditional sense, is outdated before it can be implemented. Speed—operating at real or near real-time—is pushing traditional strategy development, forecasting, competitive intelligence collection, and analysis to new limits. Vision, mission, and values are important for every organization; they shape strategy for the organization. Strategy, in turn, is influenced by information in the form of competitive intelligence. Competitive intelligence shapes vision. Due to the speed of business in the modern organization, disruptive events are prevalent. Every disruptive event ("crisis") is a violation of vision, mission, and values. Every solution to a disruptive event demands a modification, if not wholesale reworking, of strategy (vision, mission, values) and competitive intelligence activities. As the strategy and competitive intelligence disciplines come under more scrutiny, the need for a comprehensive event management system, integrated with strategy and competitive intelligence, becomes paramount. The merging of these three elements into an "integrated" business continuity process has to become a way of doing business and not existing as adjuncts to the business of the enterprise.

An effective and well adhered-to event management system integrated with strategy and competitive intelligence initiatives provides value for the organization, by allowing it to adapt rapidly to the constantly changing environment we are faced with today. The speed of response to a disruptive event will determine the outcome, either positive or negative, for the organization. The ability to connect all the elements in an organization during a disruptive event is essential for the success of the response to the event.

Value achieved through an organized response, management, and recovery effort is quantified by the intangibles—perception, information, relationships, and loyalty. Value, in some instances, cannot be seen, and often it is almost impossible to measure.

Redefining Business Continuity

Since our entry into the new millennium, many events have reshaped business continuity, as we know it. However, many business organizations have yet to refocus and comprehend the change. Y2K, for many, turned out to be a nonevent. Yes, there was a lot of hype and (seemingly) not a lot of action. In part, this may have been due to overblown media hype, fear, and lack of understanding. The ease of the Y2K transition can also be attributed to the work done by the public and private sector to identify, prevent, and mitigate the consequences of Y2K-related events. As a result, many businesses began to rethink their emphasis on traditional business continuity areas—disaster recovery, emergency response, crisis communications, crisis management, etc. Business leaders viewed these areas as "necessary evils," so to speak. They are not profit centers; they do not generate income. Like security, they are often viewed as an adjunct to the business. Then came the events of Sept. 11, 2001. The tragic events of that day should have been a wake-up call to business and government regarding the necessity for a comprehensive approach to integrated business continuity.

Herein lies the need to redefine business continuity as we know and practice it. In the introduction to this chapter and throughout this book, I cite the relationship between strategy, competitive intelligence, and event management. Recognizing this relationship, I propose the following new definition for business continuity:

All initiatives taken to assure the survival, growth and resilience of the enterprise

—Geary W. Sikich, 2002

This definition may sound very simple, but when we analyze it thoroughly and break down its component parts, the complexity of the definition becomes clear. Business continuity combines strategy, competitive intelligence, and event management into a way of doing business. Business continuity must be internalized at all levels within the organization and throughout the organization's value chain. Traditional organizational silos must be broken down; collaborative versus hierarchical decision-making, problem identification, and problem solving must take place. Business and government must recognize that they are linked and that seemingly disassociated events will have impacts requiring response, management, and recovery. Figure 3-1 depicts the linkages discussed here. Figure 3-2 illustrates the activity and information "silos" that many organizations face today.

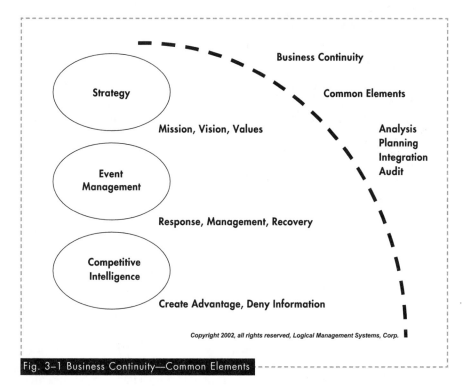

Business Continuity

Common Elements

Strategy

Mission, Vision, Values

Analysis
Planning
Integration
Audit

Event Management

Response, Management, Recovery

Competitive Intelligence

Create Advantage, Deny Information

Fig. 3–1 Business Continuity—Common Elements

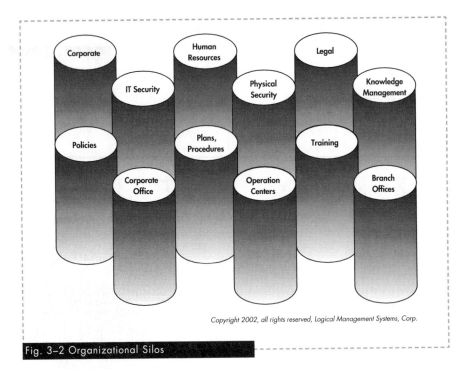

Fig. 3–2 Organizational Silos

There may be those who read the earlier text and envision chaos and indecision. The challenges of integrating strategy, competitive intelligence, and event management internally and throughout the value chain may be frustrating and seem impossible to achieve. However, when properly designed, implemented, and monitored, the integrated business continuity process actually *aids* decision-making and *lessens* chaos, confusion, and indecision. When information is shared, pre-scripted "canned responses" that do not reflect the reality of the situation at hand are no longer necessary for implementation. Dynamic decision-making, based on, as Professor Ian Mitroff has coined the phrase, "critical thinking," takes place. As Mitroff defines it:

> *Critical thinking is the ability to see problems from multiple perspectives, expose critical underlying assumptions, challenge and reverse one's assumptions, and reformulate basic arguments.*

Critical thinking is an essential ingredient as we redefine business continuity. It may seem foreign to some to see a strong relationship among strategy, competitive intelligence, and event management. However, when you practice critical thinking and "expose critical underlying assumptions," one quickly realizes that prescriptive responses are inherently static, rigid, and inflexible responses.

I use a simulation entitled, "Seven Minutes to Chaos" to get participants to practice critical thinking. The scenario is relatively simple. I tell the participants beforehand that I know without a doubt they can solve the problems caused by the disruptive events occurring in the simulation. What I ask of them—what they begin to realize as extremely difficult to accomplish—is to identify the issues and begin to develop resolution strategies for them. When this is accomplished in a collaborative environment, the results are often amazing; when it is attempted in a confrontational environment, the results are also amazing and quite devastating to the organization's ability to effectively respond to, manage, and recover from a disruptive event.

Another aspect of the new definition of business continuity is rethinking words and phrases like "crisis management." Do we really seek to "manage" crisis? What is crisis communications? What is crisis media management? I would think what we seek to do is *avoid* crisis—at all costs! *Crises* are disruptive events of such magnitude and scale that they shake an organization to its core. "Crises" carry the seeds of change with them. Unfortunately, the change that is cultivated is often as disruptive and counterproductive as the "crisis" that precipitated it.

People go out of their way to avoid crisis situations because crisis connotes conflict. If we look at conflict as a struggle to dominate, this leads to the conclusion that there is a winner and a loser in any crisis. By redefining business continuity in the manner that I have, we actually can reduce the potential for chaotic conflict resulting from a crisis. By adopting "business continuity thinking" as a way of doing business, the integration of strategy, competitive intelligence, and event management strengthen the organization's capabilities to identify potential crisis situations and circumvent them before they reach the chaotic conflict stage.

As I write this, the FBI, CIA, and other government agencies are being criticized for the September 11th events. Pundits say that the agencies knew about the flight training, that the Al-Qaida had already attempted to fly a plane into the Eiffel Tower prior to September 11th, and that we should have acted on available information. If the above is true, then it could be viewed as a perfect example of traditional business continuity thinking, i.e., hierarchical, static, silo based, and rigid.

However, to ask, "Could the events have been prevented if we had employed the definition of business continuity that I have proposed?" is a question that cannot be answered satisfactorily. In the first place, I believe that very little could have been done to prevent an incident from occurring. Second, we have just begun to experience '"terrorism" in the U.S. Third, we have yet to practice critical thinking in addressing the terrorism issue. As I pointed out in chapter 2, Executive Order 13224 does not list any domestic groups. As we reorganize the FBI and other agencies, will there be a backlash from domestic groups who feel that basic rights are being further infringed upon? Answering that question is, of course, not the focus of this book and as such I will leave it, as it is, a question for others to ponder.

As a matter of fact, properly employed, business continuity thinking can be integrated throughout the value chain, effectively reducing the potential for a disruptive event to grow to crisis proportions.

COMPONENTS OF BUSINESS CONTINUITY

The ability to effectively respond to and manage the consequences of an event in a timely manner is essential to ensure your company's survivability in today's fast-paced business environment. With the emergence of new threats—cyber- and bio-terrorism—and the increasing exposure of companies to traditional threats—fraud, systems failure, fire, explosions, spills, natural disasters, etc.—a comprehensive approach to business continuity may be your best answer.

To be effective, the approach must be vertically and horizontally integrated throughout your organization and its value chain. This approach to business continuity is based on the concept of graceful degradation and agile restoration, or what I refer to as two of the primary components of business continuity thinking. The term *graceful degradation* refers to your organization's ability to identify an event, assess its consequences, establish minimal stable functionality, devolve to the most robust less functional configuration available in the least disruptive manner possible, and begin to direct initial efforts for rapid restoration in a timely fashion. There are four principles of graceful degradation:

- Business systems are viewed as being layered, wherein the outer layer is full functionality and the inner core is minimal stable functionality
- Business systems are designed and managed to recognize when a fault occurs and gracefully devolve to the most robust less functional configuration available
- There are detectors and indicators of change from one layer to the next
- The system devolves from a fully operational state to one providing the absolute maximum stable level of service possible

The term *agile restoration* refers to your organization's ability to establish minimal stable functionality and begin controlled evolution to the most robust functional configuration available in the least disruptive manner possible, focusing on attaining full functionality in a timely fashion. There are four principles of agile restoration:

- Business systems are viewed as being layered, wherein the inner layer is minimal stable functionality and the outer layer is full functionality

- Business systems are designed and managed to recognize when opportunity for improvement occurs and effectively evolve to the next most robust functional configuration available
- There are detectors and indicators of change from one layer to the next
- Business systems evolve from absolute maximum stable level of service possible (reduced service state) to one providing the absolute maximum level of service possible (pre-event state or better)

Based on the above explanation of these two components of business continuity thinking, can you comfortably answer "yes" to the following?

- Are *all* our current business continuity commitments identified?
- Are *all* vulnerabilities, consequences, and related issues identified?
- Does our current business continuity initiative integrate strategy, competitive intelligence, and event management?
- Can I access a comprehensive event management plan for *all* types of disruptive situations?

If you are unsure of the answers or if you answered "no" to any of the questions, please read on with an open mind.

The approach to business continuity that I propose embraces consequence management as one of its key driving forces. A second key driving force is the vertical and horizontal integration of disparate "event-based" planning documents into a single plan that can be accessed for all types of disruptive events. A third key driving force is constant assessment, impact, and consequence analysis. A fourth key driving force is the integration of strategy, competitive intelligence, event response, management, and recovery. A fifth key driving force is living documentation, and a sixth key driving force is periodic validation and maintenance of all business continuity initiatives.

STRATEGY

My argument for including strategy as an element of business continuity, as defined herein, is simple and straightforward: Strategy sets the tone for the organization. From strategy evolve the initiatives driving the organization, establishing its culture, and determining the success of the enterprise. In the context of business continuity thinking, strategy must be integrated into the execution of "graceful degradation" and "agile restoration." Without strategy as a component of business continuity, devolving to the most robust less functional configuration would be extremely disruptive.

I am not going to enter a long description of what strategy is (and what it is not) in this text. There are plenty of books on business strategy you can purchase to learn all about strategy. Rather, I will illustrate the potential downside of not incorporating strategy into business continuity as defined herein. Imagine a company attempting to reorganize, restructure, or "rightsize" without a carefully thought out and executed strategy—the result would be potentially chaotic.

I once counseled a client who was about to undertake a major reorganization of business operations. They had approached me for some training on how to deal with the media. After a few careful questions to determine the scope of what they were asking for, I suggested what they really needed was a comprehensive plan to address the restructuring itself. We eventually put together a program establishing policies to address zero tolerance for workplace violence, assistance in outplacement of personnel, and training to assist personnel to recognize warning signs for workplace violence—and the training on how to talk to the media. In the end, by putting strategy and policies in place, the company was able to place the majority of its workforce in new jobs, and its restructuring of operations went forward without incident.

Without a strategy (Fig. 3-3), your organization's ability to identify events, assess their consequences, and establish minimal stable functionality without maximum disruption may be severely hampered. Without a strategy, how would you begin to direct efforts for restoration of services? Would you even know what services to restore? Don't forget about the critical infrastructures as pointed out in chapter 2. You need to develop a strategy to assure survival, growth, and resilience of the enterprise.

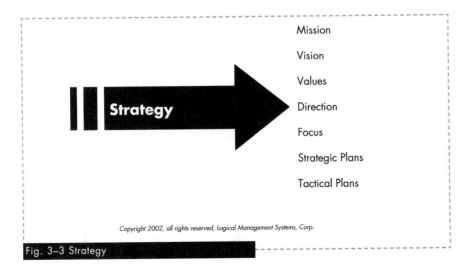

Mission

Vision

Values

Direction

Focus

Strategic Plans

Tactical Plans

Copyright 2002, all rights reserved, Logical Management Systems, Corp.

Fig. 3–3 Strategy

COMPETITIVE INTELLIGENCE

I define *competitive intelligence* as all initiatives designed to secure a competitive edge in the marketplace and all initiatives designed to deny competitive advantage to the organization's rivals. The Society of Competitive Intelligence Professionals (www.scip.org) defines competitive intelligence as:

> *A systematic and ethical program for gathering, analyzing, and managing external information that can affect your company's plans, decisions, and operations. Put another way, CI is the process of enhancing marketplace competitiveness through a greater — yet unequivocally ethical — understanding of a firm's competitors and the competitive environment.*

Competitive intelligence should be considered a very important component of business continuity. First, it allows you to achieve potential competitive advantages. This is being accomplished today by businesses entering strategic alliances that entail, as a Microsoft ad implied, "one degree of separation." If your business (or organization) is moving toward such minimal degrees of separation within your value chain, then competitive intelligence initiatives should be playing a prominent role in business continuity.

For our purposes, I define the *value chain* as the complete spectrum of relationships, touchpoints, and infrastructures on which your enterprise depends for its market success. As you can readily observe (Fig. 3-4), competitive intelligence is a significant factor in assuring business continuity.

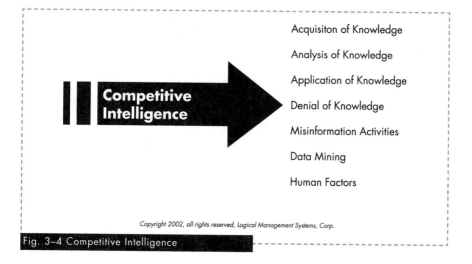

Acquisiton of Knowledge

Analysis of Knowledge

Application of Knowledge

Denial of Knowledge

Misinformation Activities

Data Mining

Human Factors

Copyright 2002, all rights reserved, Logical Management Systems, Corp.

Fig. 3-4 Competitive Intelligence

Information, no matter how well managed, is not knowledge unless it can be used. By this statement, I mean to direct your attention to the value of intelligence (information applicable to your needs) and the management of knowledge to assure business continuity. These are critical areas for business continuity. Many factors will affect competitive intelligence and knowledge management. One of them is the competitive intelligence cycle; another is how an event alters competitive intelligence activities.

It is important to understand the competitive intelligence cycle that is so critical to business success. The cycle consists of:

- collecting information
- collating information
- analyzing information
- validating information
- distributing information
- controlling information

Correct and effective assessments permit decision-makers the opportunity to effectively prioritize activities, allocate scarce resources, and manage the value chain to assure that business continuity is achieved. Intelligence collection and assessment require a broad-based effort from all elements of the organization. A planning group should, however, collate, analyze, and disseminate the final product. Examples of competitive intelligence products are:

- hazard, threat, risk analysis
- vulnerability and consequence analysis
- consequence management simulations
- location-specific intelligence packages

EVENT MANAGEMENT

The third component of business continuity is event management. The traditional approach to event management has been to "silo" the process into stand-alone plans. As a result, these plans are often not well coordinated when they have to be implemented. In addition, the plans are not comprehensive and generally lack any capability to analyze either business implications or public sector actions resulting from an event. This can be costly for an organization in today's business environment.

Building a comprehensive planning system is not difficult. In my book entitled *It Can't Happen Here: All Hazards Crisis Management Planning* (PennWell), I focused on developing a planning system based on an application of the incident command principles to the business setting. This still holds true today. Figure 3-5 summarizes the functions generally associated with an integrated event management system.

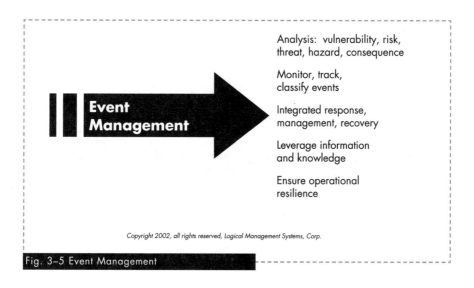

Analysis: vulnerability, risk, threat, hazard, consequence

Monitor, track, classify events

Event Management

Integrated response, management, recovery

Leverage information and knowledge

Ensure operational resilience

Copyright 2002, all rights reserved, Logical Management Systems, Corp.

Fig. 3–5 Event Management

Business decision-making and decision-application can be broken down into eight elememts. The enhanced incident command system successfully adopted by many client organizations also can be subdivided into eight parts. This may sound like an over-simplification of a complex process. However, please bear with me as I offer Table 3-1 as a simplified explanation.

Elements	Normal Business Function	Event Management Function
Management	Strategy, decision making	Strategy, decision-making
Planning	Strategic/tactical planning	Event response, mitigation, and recovery actions Assessment of competitive intelligence initiatives
Operations	Development and delivery of products, services, etc.	Mitigation of event and assessment of affected operations Prevent event from cascading to unaffected operations while continuing to develop and deliver products and services
Logistics	Ensuring that things get to where they have to be	Expediting the normal logistics operations to ensure that things get to where they have to be
Finance	Billing, payments, audit	Expediting billing, payment, and tracking of expenses
Administration	Resource management	Resource management
Infrastructure	Internal and external	Internal and external
Value chain	Suppliers, customers, stakeholders	Suppliers, customers, stakeholders

Table 3–1 Business Decision-Making and Decision-Application

I often ask clients to answer six questions as we begin an engagement. These simple questions can be very difficult for many organizations. The first question is: "What is your strategy?" It is enlightening to hear the answers. I often follow this initial question with a part-two question: "Do you know what your organization's commitments are?" Strategy (mission, vision, values) begets commitment. Many organizations have regulatory commitments they address as part of their strategy. Many do not fully comprehend their commitments.

The second question, after we have figured out their strategy, is: "What is your concept of operations?" In other words, "How are you fulfilling the commitments that you have made?"

The third question is: "Do you have the structure (organization) that serves your needs?" When we get to this question, generally some soul-searching commences. When we realize that organizations have downsized and outsourced many of the functions they used to perform internally, this question calls for a reality check.

My fourth question addresses resource management: "How are you managing your resources (human, facilities, equipment, technology, knowledge)?" Resource management is becoming very difficult for organizations as the workforce changes. Ownership of facilities and equipment is no longer seen as an asset; therefore, maintenance of non-owned facilities and equipment is in question. Managing technology has become a full-time occupation ("chief information officer" was a title not often heard in the not-too-distant past). Because of changes in corporate loyalty and workforce composition, we are facing a knowledge drain that can put a company into a difficult situation when we assess business continuity—survivability, growth, and resilience.

The fifth question hits at core competencies: "What skills do you expect from your organization?" I have consulted to organizations that had to establish and operate basic educational services for employees. Even new managers coming from a college often are required to attend extensive training designed to fill the gaps in their education. This also holds true for experienced managers. Tie this to the "knowledge" portion of question four, and you begin to see that business continuity, as we are defining it, has some difficult questions that must be answered. These answers must be communicated effectively throughout the organization's value chain and all touchpoints.

My sixth and final question: "How does your organization optimize authority, decision-making, workflow, and information sharing?" The massive modifications to business technique and systems management brought on by the information revolution cannot be overstated or under-appreciated. As traditional businesses modify their process to take advantage of the competitive benefits of technology, human resource functions are frequently overlooked. I use an analogy to determine the answer to this question. In their time, the building of pyramids and cathedrals were the biggest and most complex undertakings known. Pyramids are, however, monuments to a single person. They serve a single purpose (burial chamber) and they are non-sustaining. Cathedrals on the other hand, are self-sustaining, serve multiple purposes, and are growth engines. Sandcastles, in contrast, are built on a shifting foundation, are not made to adapt and are vulnerable to the first wave of adversity. When I describe the analogy to clients, I ask them, "Does this describe your enterprise?" after each example. It is very interesting to see the aversion to answering this question. Table 3-2 provides a breakdown of the analogy. It is an easy exercise to perform. Care to fill in the blank entitled, Your organization?

Pyramid	Monument to one	Single purpose	Nonsustaining
Cathedral	Growth engine	Multi-purpose	Self-sustaining
Sandcastle	Weak foundation	Vulnerable	Nonadaptive
Your organization	?	?	?

Table 3-2 "Does This Describe Your Enterprise?"

Your organization may exhibit characteristics of some of each of these examples. You may find pyramids built in parts of the organization. You may come across a few sandcastles. You may even come across a cathedral or two. The assessment should, however, provide an overall assessment of the entire organization as an entity.

Pyramids are companies built by and for the aggrandizement of one person. The example that readily comes to mind is a dictatorship. *Cathedrals* are self-sustaining growth engines. A cathedral requires constant care because it is being used for many purposes. The building trades that constructed the cathedral are often in demand for other projects. The example that readily comes to mind is the adaptive organization, *e.g.*, General Electric or Microsoft. *Sandcastles,* on the other hand, bring to mind the "dot-coms" and other organizations built on weak or nonexistent foundations.

FOUR PILLARS FOR EFFECTIVE BUSINESS CONTINUITY

The four pillars for successful business continuity management (Fig. 3-6) are:

Constant assessment, impact and consequence analysis

Integration of strategy, competitive intelligence, event response, management, and recovery

Living documentation

Validation and maintenance

Copyright 2002, all rights reserved, Logical Management Systems, Corp.

Fig. 3–6 Four Pillars of Business Continuity

- Constant assessment of the business environment (impact and consequence analysis)
- Integration of strategy, competitive intelligence, event response, management, and recovery into a cohesive, integrated way of doing business
- Living documentation
- Validation and maintenance

The first step to establishing a dynamic business continuity system is constant assessment. We must decide what is critical for our business to survive, grow, and exhibit resilience in the wake of events impacting the enterprise. We must define the assessment categories and determine the depth of analysis sufficiently documenting potential impacts and their consequences in relation to strategy, competitive intelligence, and event management initiatives. The assessment process is not a one-time event; it is ongoing and must be dynamic.

There are six general areas that organizations should be assessing—human factors, operations, technology, facilities, equipment, and infrastructure touchpoints.

Human factors. The area of human factors takes on new meaning when analyzing it in the context of business continuity. We have to ask ourselves questions focusing on human interaction in the assurance of strategy implementation, competitive intelligence initiatives, and event management. We need to understand the human element as we seek to determine how safe the enterprise is, *e.g.*, how well do you really know your workforce? What is the extent of background checks that are part of pre-employment screening? Can someone, either overtly, clandestinely, or unwittingly, be compromised into creating an exposure that puts the enterprise at risk? You may wish to subdivide the analysis of human factors into discreet functional areas:

- personnel security
- human resource development
- succession planning
- resource retention

Operations. Operations must be looked at from a different perspective when analyzing in the context of business continuity. We have to ask ourselves questions focusing on the operation component and its interaction with human and technology components. How will operations influence strategy implementation, competitive intelligence initiatives, and event management? We need to understand operation exposures, vulnerabilities, and consequences as we seek to determine how safe the enterprise is, *e.g.*, how long would it take to resynchronize operations and information systems? What would your organization do if your main operation was the target of a terrorist event and became a crime scene? You may wish to subdivide the analysis of operations into discreet functional areas:

- value chain vulnerability
- operations restoration time frames
- core operations (*i.e.*, "mission critical")
- continuity of operations plans
- sustainability plans

Technology. Rapid changes to technology taking place today mark this area as a challenge to analyze in the context of business continuity. We have to ask ourselves questions focusing on the interfaces, dependencies, security of systems, and interaction with human and operations components. How will technology influence strategy implementation, competitive intelligence initiatives, and event management? We need to understand technology dependencies, data storage, data corruption, security exposures, vulnerabilities, and consequences as we seek to determine how resilient the enterprise is, *e.g.,* how long would it take to recover information systems. What is the cost of downtime to your organization? What is the effect of technology investment on business continuity? You may wish to subdivide the analysis of operations into discreet functional areas:

- computer information systems plans
- account management
- configuration management
- system administration
- authentication
- network security
- cryptographic technology capability

Facilities. We hope that the events of Sept. 11, 2001 have etched into our minds the need for a comprehensive assessment of business continuity. With the possibility of the loss or extreme degradation of facilities in today's threat environment, this area becomes a critical element in the analysis process when assessing business continuity.

We have to ask ourselves questions focusing on the ability to replicate the facility environment and associated costs. How will the loss of and relocation to another facility influence strategy implementation, competitive intelligence initiatives, and event management? We need to understand facility management, security exposures, vulnerabilities, and consequences as we seek to determine how the enterprise is configured, *e.g.,* how long would it take to relocate your enterprise? What is the cost of relocation versus remote work locations? What is the effect of facility investment on business continuity? You may wish to subdivide the analysis of facilities into discreet functional areas:

- facilities recovery plan
- relocation sites for shared quarters
- facility documents/records required in emergency
- facility services
- critical requirements

Equipment. Closely associated to facilities, operations, and technology, equipment presents several challenges for analysis. We have to ask ourselves questions that focus on the ability to replicate the working environment and associated costs. How will the loss and acquisition of replacement equipment influence strategy implementation, competitive intelligence initiatives, and event management? We need to understand workstation requirements, security exposures, vulnerabilities, and consequences as we seek to determine essential items needed to keep the enterprise in business. For example, how long would it take to secure replacement equipment for your enterprise? What is the cost of replacement equipment? What is the effect of lost equipment on business continuity? You may wish to subdivide the analysis of equipment into discreet functional areas:

- copy/office machine equipment
- reprographics equipment
- specialty furniture and equipment requirements
- workstation configurations
- communications, data, voice equipment
- listings of [company] forms and supplies

Infrastructure touchpoints. As discussed in chapter 2, critical infrastructures must be identified and assessed to determine their *touchpoints* to your enterprise and what effect the loss or degradation of infrastructures may have on business continuity. Determining infrastructure impacts presents several challenges for analysis.

We have to ask ourselves questions focusing on our ability to "do without" or "make do" with reduced infrastructure reliability, *e.g.,* how will the intermittent interruption of electric supply influence strategy implementation, competitive intelligence initiatives, and event management? We need to understand infrastructure interdependencies, security exposures, vulnerabilities, and consequences of loss or degradation as we seek to determine alternatives to keep the enterprise in business, *e.g.,* how long would it take to secure generators for your enterprise? What is the cost of leasing infrastructure? What is the effect of degraded service on business continuity? You may wish to subdivide the analysis of infrastructure touchpoints into discreet functional areas:

- electrical power supplies
- energy systems (gas, oil, etc.)
- communications and data systems
- financial systems
- transportation systems
- water supply systems
- essential public sector services

In my previous books, I highlighted an assessment tool that I created called AUDITRAK^{tm}. AUDITRAK^{tm} is an assessment tool designed to provide detailed questions for the assessment of nine essential elements of analysis (EEA). These EEA are focused primarily on event management initiatives:

- administration
- event management/response organization
- event management/response system training and retraining
- facilities and equipment
- implementing procedures
- coordination with external agencies
- validation—drills and exercises
- communications
- hazard evaluation

AUDITRAK^{tm} was developed for what I will refer to as the "event management" portion of business continuity. The basis for the assessment tool is the regulatory initiatives with which many organizations have to comply. The framework for AUDITRAK^{tm} is, however, one that can be easily expanded and manipulated. The framework consists of what I term essential elements of analysis (EEA), measures of effectiveness (MOE), measures of performance (MOP), and data elements. When you decide to create your business continuity program, you can utilize this structured approach to define the assessment parameters for your organization. The ability to develop assessment tools allowing for deeper and deeper assessment can be important for an organization.

As you develop your assessment, three things should be taken into consideration:

- What do you choose to accomplish?
- What goals does the assessment activity have?
- What actions will be taken to resolve identified deficiencies?

By studying the answers to these questions, an overall strategy for assessment can be developed. The results should help to consistently improve your business continuity program. The following definitions may prove to be helpful as you develop your assessment tools.

Essential Elements of Analysis (EEA). Stand alone assessment structures encompassing a major aspect of the business continuity process. EEA when grouped together form the quantitative input for evaluation of business continuity.

Measures of Effectiveness (MOE). Subgroups of information relating to a specific area addressed by an EEA. When grouped, form the quantitative input for evaluation of an EEA.

Measures of Performance (MOP). Measurable and observable data structures forming the basis for evaluation. MOP are given a value weighting based on criticality. When grouped, form the quantitative input for evaluation of a MOE.

Data elements. Data elements are the input to the MOP queries. Data elements may take the form of numeric, yes, no, true, false, etc. responses.

In order to effectively assess business continuity initiatives, a decision-making model is necessary. Table 3-3 is an eight-point model, provided as an example of the type of decision-making model that can be created for the ongoing assessment process.

#	Process Step	End Point Result
1	Define the decision	Describe what you need to decide
2	State alternatives	Compile a list of decision alternatives
3	What are the objectives	Compile a list of the desired objectives. State them in terms of what is preferred by you in the final outcome
4	Which alternatives best meet the objectives	Evaluate each objective. Rank alternatives, one relative to another, by your opinion as to how well each would meet a single objective. Create an alphabetical ranking (A = best, B = second best, etc.)
5	Which objectives are most important	Judge the value of the objectives using the same ranking system as used for alternatives
6	Apply relative value	Combine judgment steps 4 and 5
7	Identify best choice	Add numbers across each row for alternatives
8	Make decision	Review the results; satisfying yourself that these are your best judgments

Table 3-3 Decision-Making Model

When the decision-making model is combined with the eight areas suggested for assessment and the EEA, MOE, MOP data element structure, a dynamic assessment process is created. The assessment process affords the ability to quantify assessments. As assessment results are compiled over time, comparisons can be made and adjustments to business continuity can be made.

As you apply the decision-making model you have developed, you will be able to produce a summary of potential events, probability of occurrence, and potential impact on your organization. Table 3-4 depicts this product, summarizing potential events that may threaten your organization's business continuity. When creating such a table, strongly consider the concept of graceful degradation and agile restoration with regard to the identification of critical business functions. The table you create should identify all the potential pitfalls that make up the categories of *natural*, *technical*, and *human* threats. For each threat, an estimate of the impact on critical business functions should be determined in terms of probability, impact (high, medium, low), and effect (long or short term).

The table is not meant to be comprehensive; rather, it reflects the types of events that can occur and may have a disruptive effect on your organization. Each organization should create a table custom-fitted to its particular operations; for instance, the tables for an integrated oil company and an international bank may exhibit some similarities, as should tables for other organizations and industries. Once your tables are completed, you may want to contact another industry group to see if they view the information the same way. A good method of doing this is through your local government contacts. As a matter of fact, the local government contact may find the table you have prepared to be of benefit to the community from a planning perspective.

Threats	Probability	Impact	Effect
Bomb threat			
Bomb event (culmination of the threat)			
Customer injury on premises			
Data entry threat/employee error			
Disruption of courier/delivery service			
Earthquake			
Explosion			
Fire			

Table 3–4 Disaster Exposure Rating Chart

Threats	Probability	Impact	Effect
Fraud/embezzlement			
Heating/cooling failure			
Infrastructure failure: electrical power supplies			
Infrastructure failure: energy systems (gas, oil, etc.)			
Infrastructure failure: communications and data systems			
Infrastructure failure: financial systems			
Infrastructure failure: transportation systems			
Infrastructure failure: water supply systems			
Infrastructure failure: essential public sector services			
Kidnapping/extortion			
Lightning			
Loss of critical personnel			
Natural gas leak/carbon monoxide			
Power disruption (intermittent)			
Power failure (catastrophic)			
Robbery/assault			
Snow/ice			
Software failure/virus			
Succession of key personnel			
Tampering with sensitive data			
Telecommunications failure			
Terrorist act			
Tornado/wind damage			
Unauthorized access/vandalism			
Water damage/rain storms			
Weapons of mass disruption event			
Weapons of mass destruction event			
Workplace violence			

Table 3–4 Continued . . . .

COMMUNICATING SENSITIVE INFORMATION

One of the challenges facing any organization today is the issue of communicating sensitive information. "How should it be done?" "Should we use an encryption system?" "Should we restrict access?" Your organization must answer these questions.

However, your organization may not be prepared to do so. As we redefine business continuity, we need to reassess traditional roles and responsibilities, too. Does your security division possess the background and skills necessary to address physical security as well as systems security? How should the human resources department integrate their responsibilities with the information technology and security departments?

One thing is clear: The identification, classification, encryption, and communication of sensitive information comprise an area that business continuity must be able to address in order for the organization to retain information that is considered critical. Enter the "competitive intelligence-security-human resource-information systems ultra-professional!" Oh, and you might add "strategist" and "event management planner" too!

A colleague of mine suggested that we all become "certified knowledge engineers." "What," I asked, "is a certified knowledge engineer?" He provided the following description/definition (Table 3-5).

I know what I know, because I know what I know and know that someone else knows that I know what I know

Can you meet the criteria to become a certified knowledge engineer?

- You have to know what you know

- You have to know how you know what you know

- You have to know that someone else knows that you know what you know

- If you know what it means, it makes sense. If you can get someone else to know what you meant by it, you are certified!

- I know you and so I know that not only do you know what you know but you also know what I know and this I know for sure!

As communicated to the author by Thomas B. Baines
"Certified Knowledge Engineer"

Table 3–5 Certified Knowledge Engineer

While this description may sound a bit tongue and cheek, when we begin to look at the redefinition of business continuity and the communication of sensitive information, we must begin to redefine the functions, duties, tasks, responsibilities, and interfaces of those who are responsible for the integration of these elements. I offer the following position description/definition as food for thought.

BUSINESS CONTINUITY OFFICER

This person reports to the chief executive officer and/or chief operating officer—whoever is responsible for all aspects of integrating strategy, competitive intelligence initiatives, and event management into a business continuity system for the company, including human factors, physical security, networks, systems, applications, databases, development, and telecommunications. He/she is responsible for design, product selection, implementation, and maintenance of product and architectures, including firewalls, intrusion detection, penetration testing, operations hardening, operating system hardening, remote access, virtual private networks (VPN), user authentication/PKI, access control, PBX security, and application security. Responsible for integration of strategy, competitive intelligence, and event management policies and programs, he/she is charged with development of security policies, programs, response teams, and regulatory and other compliance enforcement.

He/she assists in investigations of events as they relate to the company, both internally and externally, interfacing with senior management as necessary. Such an individual reviews business continuity components and assesses potential impacts of new projects and changes, supporting all teams within the company.

He/she requires experience in planning, issue analysis, resource development, project management, and security (physical and information systems); experience in development of policies, programs, teams, and compliance enforcement; knowledge of human factors, technology, modeling, and audit issues; and experience in leading complex programs requiring cross-functional teams and integration of corporate initiatives and experience in international regulatory issues.

In a 1997 article published on the Internet, Ian C. Jacobsen CMC, FIMC, offers the following advice on communicating sensitive information. I have summarized it here:

Sensitive information is generally important information. Careers can be at stake. I have seen both managers and employees suffer because their supervisor did not share important feedback on their interpersonal relations in time to be useful. Their almost unanimous refrain has been, "If I had known about that earlier, I could have done something about it."

Communicating sensitive information, though not pleasant, is a gesture of caring and friendship, and should be viewed as such. Here's what has worked for me:

1) Set the stage. Before you find yourself in a situation where you need to communicate sensitive information, discuss how he/she wants you to do it.

2) Get to the point quickly. People generally prefer to hear the news quickly rather than be lead to it along a suspenseful path. It also helps to describe what happened free of emotionally-charged words.

3) Test for understanding. Communicating is a closed-loop process. Test for understanding. Frequently you can pick up visual clues from the person's concentration or body language. Another way is to say, "What I have just told you is probably not what you wanted to hear. To make sure that we are on the same wavelength, please tell me what you heard." If he/she missed or misunderstood a point, you have an opportunity to clarify it.

4) Be prepared for reactions. Communicating about sensitive issues is not without risk. When we understand what normal human reactions are, we can be prepared for them. Such reactions can be:

- *Acceptance ("I didn't realize I was dominating the meetings. I'll try to change.")*

- *Defensiveness ("What do you mean that I get upset easily?")*

- *Denial ("Nicotine is not addictive!")*

- *Seeking others to blame ("I was only doing what Muriel told me to do.")*

- *Flight ("I can't deal with this now; maybe tomorrow.")*

- *"Killing the messenger" ("Since you are always criticizing the way I lead, maybe you should try working for someone else. You're fired!!")*

5) Seek help, if needed. Whether you are dealing with:

- *the person to whom you report*

- *someone who reports to you*

- *a peer or friend, or*

- *a spouse, parent, or child*

...you need to be able to communicate openly and honestly about sensitive issues. A relationship in which you can not is unhealthy; it eats away at you physically and psychologically. If you can't communicate openly with someone important to you, seek help - for both of you. If, after getting help, you still can't, you may need to re-evaluate your relationship. Life is too short to endure a relationship in which you can't communicate openly about issues that matter to you.

Communicating sensitive information generally involves multiple levels of security. These should be designed for your organization's protection and your own. Take every precaution to protect sensitive information. When you submit sensitive information via the Internet and/or Intranet, that information should be encrypted and protected with the best encryption software available. The information needs to be protected, both online and offline, using technologic and physical measures such as the following.

Physical security. Secure locations, where security personnel provide monitoring 24 hours a day, 7 days a week. Access to servers requires multiple levels of authentication.

Firewalls. Multiple levels of firewalls to filter information before reaching any web server and additional level of firewalls to protect application and database servers.

Passwords and user IDs. Keep passwords and user IDs private. No one should be able to access your password.

Account numbers and account passwords. Keep account numbers and account passwords private. When you input those items, it should be as if you have placed them in a secured lock box.

Audits and inspections. System integrity checks of the firewalls and other network perimeter access control systems should be performed on a regular, but random, basis. Your security practices and system architecture should be audited and approved by security experts and regularly upgraded to ensure that your information is completely secure.

Message board security. Message boards afford greater security than standard e-mail. This heightened security is especially important when communicating sensitive information such as bank account numbers. Communication through a message board, like all interactions, needs to be regularly audited.

Third-party sites. Links to other websites should be assessed by security for exposure vulnerabilities.

Other precautions. Examples include automatic logoff after a period of inactivity, requiring signatures for secure access to information and denial of access for security reasons after three unsuccessful log in attempts.

This is not meant to be an exhaustive discussion of how to handle sensitive information. Instead, I hope to raise the issue and communicate a sense of urgency to readers to take action to address this issue.

Issues Analysis: Critical Factors Facing Business Today

With the previous section as a teaser, let us look at the critical factors facing business today. "What are they?" depends on your particular business. However, there are some general themes that apply to any business. Here are six areas where assessment and analysis should be taking place, put into table form as a way to analyze them (Table 3-6). Each table segment is broken into the following:

- Essential elements of analysis (EEA): the area upon which analysis is being performed

- Measure of effectiveness (MOE—samples, not comprehensive): primary areas of analysis that give us indications of the overall status of the EEA

- "Crisis" definition: your definition of "crisis" for the particular MOE. For instance, under the human factors EEA/the MOE "Succession planning" might have as a crisis definition "the loss of key employees who are responsible for chief executive officer function, chief operating officer function, etc."

- Trigger point for plan activation: the event triggering the activation of the plan, e.g., the death of one or more key personnel may trigger the activation of the succession plan. I have generally found that six categories establish trigger points: life safety impact, infrastructures, operational status, facility occupancy, corporate impact, and actions. A more detailed discussion of trigger points and event classification will be presented in a later chapter

- Position responsible for assessment: the position within your organization with responsibility for completing the earlier items and for the comprehensive assessment and analysis of the EEA. There may be many positions and departments having input to the assessment; however, a single point of contact should maintain responsibility for compiling and analyzing the information and determining its meaning to the organization

Take some time to complete the information presented in the accompanying table. You should be able to add more MOE details as you focus each area on your organization's particular requirements.

Essential Elements of Analysis: Human Factors			
Measure of Effectiveness	"Crisis" Definition	Trigger Point for Plan Activation	Position Responsible for Assessment
Personnel security			
Human resource development			
Succession planning			
Resource retention			

Essential Elements of Analysis: Operations			
Measure of Effectiveness	"Crisis" Definition	Trigger Point for Plan Activation	Position Responsible for Assessment
Value chain vulnerability			
Operations restoration time frames			
Core operations (i.e., mission critical)			
Continuity of operations plans			
Sustainability plans			

Essential Elements of Analysis: Technology			
Measure of Effectiveness	"Crisis" Definition	Trigger Point for Plan Activation	Position Responsible for Assessment
Computer plans			
Account management			
Configuration management			
Authentication			
Network security			
Cryptographic technology capability			
System administration			

Table 3–6 Essential Element of Analysis: Example Assessment

Essential Elements of Analysis: Facilities

Measure of Effectiveness	"Crisis" Definition	Trigger Point for Plan Activation	Position Responsible for Assessment
Facilities recovery plan			
Relocation sites for shared quarters			
Facility documents/ records required in emergency			
Facility services			
Critical requirements			

Essential Elements of Analysis: Equipment

Measure of Effectiveness	"Crisis" Definition	Trigger Point for Plan Activation	Position Responsible for Assessment
Copy/office machine equipment			
Reprographics equipment			
Specialty furniture and equipment requirements			
Workstation configurations			
Communications, data, voice equipment			
Listings of [company] forms and supplies			

Essential Elements of Analysis: Infrastructure Touchpoints

Measure of Effectiveness	"Crisis" Definition	Trigger Point for Plan Activation	Position Responsible for Assessment
Electrical power supplies			
Energy systems (gas, oil, etc.)			
Communications and data systems			
Financial systems			
Transportation systems			
Water supply systems			
Essential public sector services			

Table 3–6 Continued . . .

Concluding Thoughts

In this chapter, we discussed the relationship between your organization's strategy, competitive intelligence initiatives, and event management as they apply to an overall concept of business continuity. Included were examples of how the overall concept of business continuity integrates strategy, competitive intelligence, and event management. We discussed the key steps to applying the overall concept of business continuity to an organization:

- analysis and assessment
- business continuity plan
- competitive intelligence impacts during a "crisis"
- communicating sensitive information
- issues analysis—critical factors facing business today

This chapter is intended to build upon your assessment of potential risks, hazards, threats, vulnerabilities, and their consequences. After reading this chapter, you should be able to apply the concepts discussed to develop for your organization a structure and business continuity concepts at all levels within your organization and its value chain.

References

Davis, Stanley M., Christopher Meyer, *Blur: The Speed of Change in the Connected Economy*, 1998

Executive Order 13224 - Blocking Property and Prohibiting Transactions With Persons Who Commit, Threaten to Commit, or Support Terrorism can be found at www.ustreas.gov/terrorism

Jacobson, Ian, C., Communicating Sensitive Information, Internet Article, 1997

Microsoft advertisement describing 1° of separation, 2001

Mitroff, Ian, I. Avoid "E3" Thinking, Management General, 1998

———Smart Thinking for Crazy Times: The Art of Solving the Right Problems, 1998

Society for Competitive Intelligence Professionals (SCIP), Definition of Competitive Intelligence, (www.scip.org)

Sikich, Geary W. It Can't Happen Here: All Hazards Crisis Management Planning, PennWell Publishing, 1993

———Logical Management Systems, Corp. AUDITRAK™ Diagnostic Assessment Program (www.logicalmanagement.com)

———What is there to know about a crisis, John Liner Review, vol. 14, no. 4, Winter 2001

———Graceful Degradation and Agile Restoration, White Paper, Logical Management Systems, Corp., March 2002

———Graceful Degradation and Agile Restoration Synopsis, Disaster Resource Guide, 2002

———Business Continuity in Times of Uncertainty: Building Pyramids, Cathedrals or Sandcastles, Disaster Recovery Journal Fall Conference, September 2002

Chapter Four

YOUR NEXT "CRISIS:" IDENTIFYING TIME-CRITICAL ISSUES

Chapter Summary

In this chapter, we will discuss *time-critical issues*—issues that, if affected by a disruptive event, cause an immediate "crisis" for your enterprise. They are also the issues having the most immediate impact on your enterprise.

Included are examples of time-critical issues that affect your enterprise, including but not limited to:

- loss of critical infrastructures
- telecommunications/information systems
- transportation (air, land, water)
- utilities (gas, electric, water)
- energy supply
- critical services
- access denial

DEFINITION OF TERMS USED IN THIS CHAPTER

Time-critical
Time frame of reference for determining crisis

Classification system
Trigger points for activation of plan

- degradation/loss of critical operations
- loss/degradation of operational capability
- loss of electrical supply sources
- loss of telecommunications/information sources
- loss/degradation of buildings/occupancy
- disruption of transportation
- disruption of water supply
- disruption of emergency services

This chapter is intended to help you to identify crises, assess the consequences of loss, and provide a basis for mitigation planning should an event occur where you lose one or more of the time-critical issues discussed herein. The outcome you should achieve is a concept for the structure and application of your business continuity process for addressing the consequences of time-critical issues at various levels of your organization. We will also expand your assessment and analysis initiatives, so that you should better understand potential vulnerabilities that your organization faces and how to quantify its time-critical issues. You should also be able to determine the consequences of a disruptive event relating to time-critical issues.

Time-critical. The loss of any business function, related value-chain component, internal and/or external infrastructures, such that the result of that loss poses an imminent threat to the survival of the enterprise.

Classification system. A system for determining the severity of an event utilizing a unique set of criteria to define and measure the level of severity of the event.

Introduction

We are all conscious of time in today's business world. Everything from "just-in-time" delivery, to production and distribution, to the speed of information processing is based on time. Business continuity, as defined, is also based on time. Time is a factor. "Time will tell" if your organization grows, prospers, survives, and is resilient to disruptive events. When developing the concept of business continuity thinking, time was a critical factor.

I am going to introduce concepts, addressing how one can determine what is "time-critical" to the organization. The definition may vary slightly from organization to organization. However, for our purposes, we will define time-critical as:

> *The loss of any business function, related value-chain component, internal and/or external infrastructures, such that the result of that loss poses an imminent threat to the survival of the enterprise.*

In the chapter overview, I provided a list of potential time-critical issues. Figure 4-1 depicts some of the potential events that organizations face today. We will discuss each and provide examples of analysis tools you can use to determine how these may be time-critical to your organization.

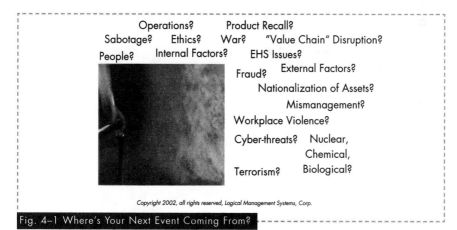

Operations?   Product Recall?
Sabotage?   Ethics?   War?   "Value Chain" Disruption?
People?   Internal Factors?   EHS Issues?
Fraud?   External Factors?
Nationalization of Assets?
Mismanagement?
Workplace Violence?
Cyber-threats?   Nuclear,
Chemical,
Terrorism?   Biological?

Copyright 2002, all rights reserved, Logical Management Systems, Corp.

Fig. 4–1 Where's Your Next Event Coming From?

Time-Critical Events

Table 4-1 is a survey designed to determine how well prepared you and your organization are to respond to, manage, and recover from a time-critical event.

	Yes	No
Is your organization prepared to respond to, manage, and recover from a time-critical event?		
Has your organization ever experienced a time-critical event?		
Do you think it might someday experience a time-critical event?		
Have you ever played a part in managing an event (crisis)?		
Have you participated in managing a crisis you thought could have been handled more effectively with greater preparation?		
Are you concerned that your organization is vulnerable to a time-critical event?		
Are your instincts telling you that something should be done now to help your organization prevent events from occurring or escalating in severity?		
Are you sometimes confused by the advice you read or are given on event management?		
Do you have the authority to take action to implement an event management program within your organization?		

Evaluation:

0–3 "Yes" answers—Your business is more fortunate than most or you might be underestimating the potential for an event in your business
4–6 "Yes" answers—Your business is vulnerable to an event.
If it hasn't occurred already, you're quite fortunate
6–8 "Yes" answers—You've probably lived through one or more crises, or will experience an event soon. You are likely in a business extremely vulnerable to events that can easily turn into a crisis

Table 4–1 Time-Critical Event Survey

Based on your answers, you may or may not have a feel for your organization's ability to respond to, manage, and recover from a time-critical event. The next step in the development process is to identify the time-critical events for your organization. Once we have a list of time-critical events we can begin to analyze them to determine the common effects that these events would trigger. *Analysis* is the process of measuring performance against a set of criteria to provide a meaningful rendering of data indicating the level of ability required to accomplish tasks that have been committed to. I have used the LMSCARVER™ analysis tool (with modifications) to assist clients in determining effective strategies for time-critical event response, management, mitigation and recovery operations. We will discuss the application of LMSCARVER™ in subsequent sections of this chapter.

TIME-CRITICAL—EFFECTS ON BUSINESS CONTINUITY

Let us start by taking a quiz (Table 4-2) that I often use with clients as a method of getting them to think about business continuity in a broader perspective. The quiz is relatively simple and it is easy to score. In order to get full point values for a question, you must answer the entire question "yes." There are several questions asking for answers to specific sub-elements. If you answer "no" to any of the sub-elements, you should score the entire question as having been answered "no." This may sound a bit draconian; however, you will see that the questions are designed to interrelate to each other, and for those questions with multiple elements, this interrelationship aspect is important. You may think that I should have made each a separate question, but I have found that if one area gets a "no" answer, then the other areas are probably going to get a "no" answer also. The reality is that if you have not addressed one of the sub-elements—even if you think you have addressed others—most likely you have not really addressed the main element.

Questions 3 and 4 relate to topics for the next two chapters. You may wish to consider reviewing your answers to these questions once you have read them. Additionally, this chapter provides forms, questionnaires, and other tools applicable to the material covered in the next two chapters. I have chosen not to reproduce the forms, questionnaires, etc. in the next two chapters as this may prove less confusing to the reader if they are contained in one chapter. You can apply these tools to the next two chapters easily enough.

#		Yes	No
1	Have written standards for management performance been established?		
2	Has your organization identified time-critical functions, that if disrupted for 0-3 days could create a crisis?		
3	Has your organization identified time-sensitive functions, that if disrupted for 4-7 days could create a crisis?		
4	Has your organization identified its time-dependent functions, that if disrupted for 8+ days could create a crisis?		
5	Does your organization depend on external resources to support business functions?		
6	Could the loss of a core business function cascade throughout your organization?		
7	Does your organization have adequate funds in reserve or access to capital resources to operate for a period of 30 days?		
8	Has a specific business continuity management plan (BCMP) been developed for each business process?		
9	Does the BCMP address the loss of the following critical infrastructures/services:		
	Telecommunications and information systems		
	Utilities (electric, gas, water)		
	Energy sources/supply		
	Financial and capital resources		
	Vital human resources and services		
	Transportation services		
	Value chain services and resources (suppliers, customers, etc.)		
	External services and resources (medical, government, etc.)		
10	Is the BCMP integrated, cross-referenced, and indexed?		
11	Does the BCMP address the following six critical functions:		
	Management decision making		
	Planning (tactical, strategic, competitive intelligence)		
	Operations (time-critical, time-sensitive, time-dependent)		
	Logistics (near-term, long-term, vendors, suppliers)		
	Finance (capital on-hand, capital for 30 days operations)		
	Administration (critical human resources and services)		
12	Is there a single point of authority for the coordination of the BCMP?		
13	Has your organization conducted simulations (drills) to validate the BCMP?		
14	Are all commitments made in the BCMP:		
	Identified		
	Documented		
	Verified		
15	Does the BCMP address the following steps and establish time frames in the response/recovery process for:		
	initial response strategies, including classification of incident		
	activation of alternate strategies and sites		
	restoration of critical processes		
	infrastructure restoration		
	information recovery and synchronization		
	full function restoration		
	permanent restoration		

Table 4–2 Business Continuity Quiz—Time-Critical Issues

Once you have completed the quiz, tally your answers and the points generated on the form below (Table 4-3). The goal here is an honest representation of your organization's business continuity capabilities.

If you answered honestly, the score will give you a snapshot of where your organization stands regarding business continuity. A high score does not mean you can rest on your laurels, and a low score does not mean you have to reorganize

Question #	Point Value	Yes	No
1	6		
2	6		
3	6		
4	6		
5	6		
6	6		
7	6		
8	6		
9	10		
10	6		
11	9		
12	6		
13	6		
14	6		
15	9		
Total	100		

Table 4–3 Answer Form

and blister through an accelerated development process. The score is subjective and the quiz is designed to get you thinking about issues—some of them you have little control over, by the way!

The quiz is illustrative of the need for business continuity to broaden the scope of its definition. Each of the questions and your answers has a strategy component, a competitive intelligence component, and an event management component. Unless you assess the questions against these three components, your answers will not be reflective of how your organization is currently addressing business continuity. While I will not attempt to dissect each question against the three components, it may be illustrative to do an example question.

Let's take question 11 and assess it against the three components—strategy, competitive intelligence, and event management (Table 4-4). Question 11 asks:

> Does your business continuity management plan address six critical functions: Management decision-making, planning (tactical, strategic, competitive intelligence), operations (time-critical, time-sensitive, time-dependent), logistics (near-term, long-term, vendors, suppliers), finance (capital on hand, capital for 30 days operations) and administration (critical human resources and services).

Assessment Area	Strategy	Competitive Intelligence	Event Management
Management	Creation of strategic vision (mission, vision, values) Decision making to guide the organization to achieve its mission, grow, survive, and ensure resilience	Application of information in the form of intelligence and knowledge to further the creation of strategic vision	Decision making to facilitate alterations to strategic vision and ensure that mission, vision, and values are not compromised during the event
Planning	Analysis of mission, vision, values to create tactical (near-term) plans and strategic (long-term) plans	Acquisition information that can be used to gain a competitive advantage and ensure the execution of strategy Denial of information to competitors to assure competitive advantage	Assessment of vulnerabilities created by the event that will result in information becoming available to competitors Development of plans to mitigate and minimize the effects of the event
Operations	Execution of strategy to produce goods, services, and create value	Security measures taken to reduce exposure to competitors' attempts to gain information	Event response, management, and recovery efforts Prevention of event cascading to nonaffected operations
Logistics	Enterprise resource identification, management, and monitoring	Security measures taken to reduce exposure to competitors' attempts to gain information	Support of affected operations, streamlining logistics processes, and implementation of out of normal logistics procedures
Finance	Establishing market value for goods and services, tracking costs, profits, and auditing cash-flow	Security measures taken to reduce exposure to competitors' attempts to gain information	Event cost tracking, expediting cost accounting, and implementing cost control measures and audit procedures
Administration	Creation of policies, procedures, and resource applications to achieve strategy	Security measures taken to reduce exposure to competitors' attempts to gain information	Assuring resource availability, allocation, and management Record keeping, documentation, policy and procedure modification, development, and implementation

Table 4–4 Strategy, Competitive Intelligence, and Event Management

Table 4-4 is not meant to provide an exhaustive analysis of question 11, but to provide examples of how the three components are linked in the context of business continuity. I have found it useful to assign responsibility for the identification, collection, analysis, distribution, and management of the information generated from the business continuity process. Table 4-5 is an example of this process.

Management Issues	Resources Required	Responsible Party
Establishing direction for the organization (vision) Defining how the organization will achieve its vision (mission) Establishing the culture and ethics that the organization adheres to (values)	Management committee Board of directors Legal counsel	Chief executive officer
Planning Issues	**Resources Required**	**Responsible Party**
Creating strategy to achieve the goals of the organization (near and long term)	Risk management Strategic planning Human resources Compliance/audit	Chief financial officer
Operations Issues	**Resources Required**	**Responsible Party**
Implementation of strategy into value for the organization (products, services, etc.)	Operations Engineering Safety, environmental Quality assurance	Chief operating officer
Logistics Issues	**Resources Required**	**Responsible Party**
Resource identification, acquisition, management, and replenishment	Supply chain Enterprise resource planning Purchasing	Controller/purchasing
Finance Issues	**Resources Required**	**Responsible Party**
Establishing and maintaining budgets, controlling costs, distribution of financial resources, and collection of debts for services rendered	Accounting Billing Collection Legal Audit	Chief financial officer
Administration Issues	**Resources Required**	**Responsible Party**
Identification and management of resources (human, facilities, and equipment)	Facilities Records management Internal infrastructure Subject matter experts	Human resource executive

Table 4–5 Assigning Responsibility for Business Continuity Processes

Infrastructure Issues	Resources Required	Responsible Party
Identification of internal and external infrastructures supporting the core business processes, information processing, and management All security measures (physical, cyber)	Information technology Security Subject matter experts	Chief information officer

External Issues	Resources Required	Responsible Party
Identification and management of all stakeholder issues relating to the organization	Public affairs Legal counsel Subject matter experts	Public and governmental affairs

Value Chain Issues	Resources Required	Responsible Party
Identification and management of all components of the value chain (customers, suppliers, vendors, regulators, and vested interests)	Customers Vendors Suppliers Other stakeholders	Chief operating officer

Other Issues	Resources Required	Responsible Party
Clearinghouse function for identification, screening, and coordination of issues, management relating to organizational direction, growth, survival, and resilience	Business intelligence sources Subject matter experts Associations Other information sources	Chief security officer

Table 4–5 Continued . . .

Your organization needs to structure a similar table reflecting your structure and the responsible titles. This is a useful exercise, because the results achieved can enhance business continuity and facilitate cooperation within the organization throughout the value chain.

Once you have completed Table 4-5, your organization can begin to assess the time-critical aspects of events. Table 4-6 is an example of events that could occur to any organization. The key to completing the table is determining the time-critical consequences and effects resulting from the occurrence of an event. I generally use a series of time frames to determine time-critical consequences and effects for clients. It is important to note that time frames will vary from organization to organization and within the organization. General Motors learned this lesson when it had to halt production as a result of one of its suppliers being unable to deliver the parts needed.

Event	Probability (H,M,L)			Impact (H,M,L)			Time-Critical Consequences	Effect: "Crisis" Trigger Point
Loss of critical internal infrastructures								
Loss of critical external infrastructures								
Voice, data, information systems								
Transportation (air, land, water)								
Utilities (gas, electric, water)								
Energy supply								
Critical services								
Access denial								
Degradation/loss of critical Operations								
Loss/degradation of operational capability								
Loss of electrical supply sources								
Loss of voice, data, information sources								
Loss/degradation of buildings/occupancy								
Disruption of transportation								
Disruption of water supply								
Disruption of emergency services								
Other: describe any event not listed above								

Table 4–6 Events That Could Occur to Any Organization

Once you have completed this assessment, you should have a pretty good idea of the time-critical parameters (time from occurrence to "crisis") for your organization. The next step is to begin to categorize time-critical events into manageable clusters—in other words, a list of "worst-case" scenarios.

A word of caution: Worst-case scenarios—theoretical sequences of events intentionally devised to be as bad as possible—are creative exercises, not predictions of likely events. Therefore, you need to explore the realities of your world by developing "most likely case" scenarios. Most likely case scenarios are also theoretical sequences of events, but are intentionally devised to reflect known outcomes. Most likely case scenarios are also creative exercises, based on what has happened in the past. We discussed the LMSCARVER™

analysis process in chapter 2; this process was developed to assist clients in the creation of vulnerability assessments. The components are:

C = Critical

A = Accessible

R = Recognizable

V = Vulnerable

E = Effect

R = Recoverable

The LMSCARVER™ principles can be applied to further refine your assessment of time-critical events. Your goal will be to eventually develop a series of tables describing time-critical events for your organization as depicted in Table 4-7.

Highly likely to occur:	
1.	
2.	
3.	
4.	
5.	
Could occur, but unlikely in the near term:	
1.	
2.	
3.	
4.	
5.	
Is Unlikely to occur:	
1.	
2.	
3.	
4.	
5.	

Table 4–7 Possible Time-Critical Situations—Probability of Occurrence

Once you have completed the initial listing of possible time-critical events based on probability of occurrence, you need to assess the impact on your business operations. You should take the lists and work them into the next set of tables (Table 4-8).

Would have serious impact:	
1.	
2.	
3.	
4.	
5.	
Would have impact, but could be managed:	
1.	
2.	
3.	
4.	
5.	
Would have little impact and could be managed easily:	
1.	
2.	
3.	
4.	
5.	

Table 4–8 Possible Time-Critical Situations—Impact on the Business

Now that you have established a rank ordering of the events that could occur and ranked them by impact on the business, you can further assess them against Table 4-9. The goal is to define the time-critical events that are of the highest priority and will require the most resources to address from a planning, response, management, and recovery perspective.

Highly likely to occur/would have serious impact:	
1.	
2.	
3.	
4.	
5.	
Highly likely to occur/would have impact, but could be managed:	
1.	
2.	
3.	
4.	
5.	
Could occur, but unlikely in the near term/would have serious impact:	
1.	
2.	
3.	
4.	
5.	

Table 4-9 Possible Time-Critical Situations—Most Likely and Greatest Impact

Once you have completed the three-part process using the LMSCARVER™ principles, you will have narrowed your list down based on *probability of occurrence* and *impact to the business*. With this information, you can begin to develop some proactive measures addressing the time-critical events that could put your organization into a crisis, disrupt business continuity, and potentially threaten survival of the organization.

This can be accomplished by completing Table 4-10 for each of the time-critical events you have identified. The goal here is to determine how to best minimize the impact of a time-critical event so that your organization can effectively respond to, manage, and recover from the event without significantly disrupting the business. I focus on minimizing the effect instead of eliminating the event. That is partially because I believe you cannot eliminate all events occurring, but you can do a lot to minimize their effects.

Table 4-10 is an example of how to address a time-critical event.

Time-Critical Event	Prevention Measures	Proactive Action Step
Loss of electrical supply	Purchase generators to serve as alternate source of electric power	Assign responsibility Assess costs Prepare purchase and service orders
	Purchase uninterruptible power source (UPS) for information technology assets	Obtain equipment Install and test equipment
	Purchase emergency supply of flashlights, batteries and candles to provide temporary light source	Perform routine maintenance on equipment Document for planning purposes

Table 4–10 How to Address a Time-Critical Event

In keeping with the theme of this chapter, Table 4-11 is provided to facilitate the thought process and aid in the development of your time-critical inventory of events.

Remember that you have to look at the complete network in which your organization operates. Once you identify the particulars of the network, you can begin to define the touchpoints for your organization and the potential time-critical events that you will need to address in your business continuity plan.

Time-Critical Issues for Analysis	What makes this a time-critical issue?
Loss of critical infrastructures	
Telecommunications/information systems	
Transportation (air, land, water)	
Disruption of emergency services	
Utilities (gas, electric, water)	
Energy supply	
Critical services	
Access denial	
Degradation/loss of critical operations	
Loss/degradation of operational capability	
Loss of electrical supply sources	
Loss of telecommunications/information sources	
Loss/degradation of buildings/occupancy	
Disruption of transportation	
Disruption of water supply	

Table 4–11 Thinking Through Development of Time-Critical Elements

Concluding Thoughts

When looking at time-critical events, you need to take into account strategy, competitive intelligence initiatives, and event management as they relate to how your organization will address these issues.

We have included examples of how best to assess time-critical events and some that your organization may wish to consider as starting points for assessment and analysis.

As with previous chapters, this is intended to build upon your assessment capabilities. You should be able to apply these concepts to develop a listing of time-critical events that would have potential impacts at all levels within your organization and its value chain.

References

Caponigro, Jeffrey, R. *The Crisis Counselor*, 1998

Sikich, Geary W. "Business Continuity in Times of Uncertainty: Building Pyramids, Cathedrals or Sandcastles," *Disaster Recovery Journal* Fall Conference, September 2002

Chapter Five

THE SMOLDERING "CRISIS:" TIME-SENSITIVE ISSUES

Chapter Summary

In this chapter, we will discuss *time-sensitive issues*—issues that, if left to smolder, will sneak up and cause a "crisis" for your enterprise. They are also the issues having both long- and short-term impacts on your enterprise. Included are examples of time-sensitive issues that can affect your enterprise. These issues include, but are not limited to:

- financial issues
- vendor/supplier
- business applications
- human resources and staffing
- legal oversight/documentation
- transition to recovery organization
- recovery operations
- humanitarian assistance

DEFINITION OF TERMS USED IN THIS CHAPTER

Time-sensitive
Time frame of reference for determining crisis

Classification system
Trigger points for activation of plan

- infrastructure restoration
- information and operations recovery and synchronization
- resumption of critical business functions
- full function restoration
- permanent restoration

This chapter is intended to help you to identify and assess the consequences of loss, and provide a basis for "mitigation planning," should an event occur in which you lose one or more of the time-sensitive elements discussed. The outcome you should achieve is a concept for the structure and application of your business continuity management plan for addressing the consequences of time-sensitive issues at various levels of your organization.

Time-sensitive. The loss of any business function, related value chain component, internal and/or external infrastructures, the result of which loss poses a near-term threat to the survival of the enterprise.

Classification system. A system for determining the severity of an event utilizing a unique set of criteria to define and measure the level of severity of the event.

Introduction

In the previous chapter, I introduced the concept of "time-critical;" here, I am going to continue to address "time issues." For our purposes, we will define *time-sensitive* as:

> *The loss of any business function, related value chain component, internal and/or external infrastructures, such that the result of that loss poses a near-term threat to the survival of the enterprise.*

The chapter overview provided a list of potential time-sensitive areas. We will discuss each and expand on the analytical tools presented in the previous chapter. You will be able to use these tools to determine time-sensitive issues for your organization.

Time-Sensitive Events

Previously, I asked you to take a survey to determine how well prepared you and your organization are to respond to, manage, and recover from a time-critical event. Here, we will take the same survey, only this time we will focus on time-sensitive events (Table 5-1).

	Yes	No
Is your organization prepared to respond to, manage, and recover from a time-sensitive event?		
Has your organization ever experienced a time-sensitive event?		
Do you think it might someday experience a time-sensitive event?		
Have you ever played a part in managing an event (crisis)?		
Have you participated in managing a crisis that you thought could have been handled more effectively with greater preparation?		
Are you concerned that your organization is vulnerable to a time-sensitive event?		
Are your instincts telling you that something should be done now to help your organization prevent events from occurring or escalating in severity?		
Are you sometimes confused by the advice you read or are given on event management?		
Do you have the authority to take action to implement an event management program within your organization?		

Evaluation:

0–3 "Yes" answers—Your business is more fortunate than most or you might be underestimating the potential for an event in your business
4–6 "Yes" answers—Your business is vulnerable to an event.
If it hasn't occurred already, you're quite fortunate
6–8 "Yes" answers—You've probably lived through one or more crises, or will experience an event soon. You are likely in a business extremely vulnerable to events that can easily turn into a crisis

Table 5–1 Time-Sensitive Event Survey

Your answers in the previous chapter, coupled with your answers in this one, may offer you a better understanding regarding your organization's ability to respond to, manage, and recover from time-critical and time-sensitive events. The next step, as in the previous chapter, is to identify time-sensitive events for your organization. Once you have a list of time-sensitive events, you can begin to analyze them to determine the common effects these events would trigger. Using the LMSCARVER™ analysis tool with modifications to fit your organization, you can determine effective strategies for time-sensitive event response, management, mitigation, and recovery operations. We will again discuss the application of LMSCARVER™ in subsequent sections.

TIME-SENSITIVE—EFFECTS ON BUSINESS CONTINUITY

Take the quiz I introduced in the previous chapter, but this time answer the questions in relation to "time-sensitive" events (Table 5-2). As in the previous chapter, in order to get full point values for a question, you must answer the entire question "yes." As a reminder, there are several questions asking for answers to specific sub-elements. If you answer "no" to any one of the sub-elements, you should score the entire question as having been answered "no."

Questions 3 and 4 have been modified to relate to the topics from the previous chapter and for the next chapter. You may wish to consider reviewing your answers to these questions once you have read the next chapter. I will not introduce new forms for analysis in this chapter; rather I will use the forms from the previous chapter to further the analysis process.

#		Yes	No
1	Have written standards for management performance been established?		
2	Has your organization identified time-critical functions that if disrupted for 0-3 days could create a crisis? (If you answer no, you did not read the last chapter!)?		
3	Has your organization identified time-sensitive functions that if disrupted for 4-7 days could create a crisis?		
4	Has your organization identified its time-dependent functions that if disrupted for 8+ days could create a crisis?		
5	Does your organization depend on external resources to support business functions?		
6	Could the loss of a core business function cascade throughout your organization ?		
7	Does your organization have adequate funds in reserve or access to capital resources to operate for a period of 30 days?		
8	Has a specific business continuity management plan (BCMP) been developed for each business process?		
9	Does the BCMP address the loss of the following critical infrastructures/services:		
	Telecommunications and information systems		
	Utilities (electric, gas, water)		
	Energy sources/supply		
	Financial and capital resources		
	Vital human resources and services		
	Transportation services		
	Value chain services and resources (suppliers, customers, etc.)		
	External services and resources (medical, government, etc.)		
10	Is the BCMP integrated, cross-referenced, and indexed?		
11	Does the BCMP address the following six critical functions:		
	Management decision making		
	Planning (tactical, strategic, competitive intelligence)		
	Operations (time-critical, time-sensitive, time-dependent)		
	Logistics (near-term, long-term, vendors, suppliers)		
	Finance (capital on-hand, capital for 30 days operations)		
	Administration (critical human resources and services)		
12	Is there a single point of authority for the coordination of the BCMP?		
13	Has your organization conducted simulations (drills) to validate the BCMP?		
14	Are all commitments made in the BCMP:		
	Identified		
	Documented		
	Verified		
15	Does the BCMP address the following steps and establish time frames in the response/recovery process for:		
	initial response strategies, including classification of incident		
	activation of alternate strategies and sites		
	restoration of critical processes		
	infrastructure restoration		
	information recovery and synchronization		
	full function restoration		
	permanent restoration		

Table 5–2 Business Continuity Quiz—Time-Sensitive Issues

Once you have completed the quiz, tally your answers and the points generated on the form below (Table 5-3). The goal is an honest representation of your organization's business continuity capabilities.

Question #	Point Value	Yes	No
1	6		
2	6		
3	6		
4	6		
5	6		
6	6		
7	6		
8	6		
9	10		
10	6		
11	9		
12	6		
13	6		
14	6		
15	9		
Total	100		

Table 5-3 Scoring

Compare your answers with the score you had when you took the quiz in the last chapter. How do your answers regarding time-sensitive issues vary from your answers for time-critical issues?

As you did in the previous chapter, create a table identifying the issue, resources required, and responsible party. I recommend you complete this useful exercise for time-sensitive issues as you did for time-critical issues. The results should provide you further direction for the development of business continuity within your organization.

As previously, once you have completed the table, your organization can begin to assess the time-sensitive aspects of events. Table 5-4 (also provided in the last chapter) is an example of events that could occur to any organization. Complete this table determining the time-sensitive consequences and effects that would result from the occurrence of an event. As with time-critical events, I use a series of time frames to determine time-sensitive consequences and effects for clients. As mentioned in the last chapter, these time frames will vary from organization to organization and within the organization.

Event	Probability (H,M,L)			Impact (H,M,L)			Time - Sensitive Consequences	Effect: "Crisis" Trigger Point
Financial issues								
Vendor/supplier								
Business applications								
Human resources and staffing								
Legal								
Oversight/documentation								
Transition to recovery organization								
Recovery operations								
Humanitarian assistance								
Infrastructure restoration								
Information recovery and synchronization								
Information and operations synchronization								
Resumption of critical business functions								
Full function restoration								
Permanent restoration								
Other: describe any event not listed above								

Table 5–4 Events That Could Occur to Any Organization

Once you have completed this assessment, you should have a pretty good idea of the time-sensitive parameters (time from occurrence to crisis) for your organization. As with time-critical events, your next step is to categorize the time-sensitive events into manageable clusters. Using the LMSCARVER™ principles, you can refine your assessment of time-sensitive events. Develop a series of tables describing time-sensitive events for your organization as depicted in Table 5-5.

Highly likely to occur:	
1.	
2.	
3.	
4.	
5.	
Could occur, but unlikely in the near term:	
1.	
2.	
3.	
4.	
5.	
Is Unlikely to occur:	
1.	
2.	
3.	
4.	
5.	

Table 5–5 Possible Time-Sensitive Situations—Probability of Occurrence

Once you have completed the initial listing of possible time-sensitive events based on probability of occurrence, you need to assess the impact on your business operations. Take the lists and work them into Table 5-6.

Would have serious impact:	
1.	
2.	
3.	
4.	
5.	
Would have impact, but could be managed:	
1.	
2.	
3.	
4.	
5.	
Would have little impact and could be managed easily:	
1.	
2.	
3.	
4.	
5.	

Table 5–6 Possible Time-Sensitive Situations—Impact on the Business

Now that you have established a rank ordering of the time-sensitive events that could occur and ranked them by impact on the business, you can further assess them against Table 5-7. The goal is to identify and define time-sensitive events that are of the highest priority and will require the most resources to address from a planning, response, management, and recovery perspective.

	Highly likely to occur/would have serious impact:
1.	
2.	
3.	
4.	
5.	
	Highly likely to occur/would have impact, but could be managed:
1.	
2.	
3.	
4.	
5.	
	Could occur, but unlikely in the near term/would have serious impact:
1.	
2.	
3.	
4.	
5.	

Table 5–7 Highest Priority Time-Sensitive Situations—Most Likely and Greatest Impact

Once you have completed the three-part process using the LMSCARVER™ principles, you will have narrowed your list of time-sensitive events down based on probability of occurrence and impact to the business. With this information, you can begin to develop some proactive measures addressing the time-sensitive events that could put your organization into a crisis, disrupt business continuity, and potentially threaten survival of the organization.

As previously, complete Table 5-8 for each of the time-sensitive events that you have identified. The goal is to determine how to best minimize the impact of a time-sensitive event so that your organization can effectively respond to, manage, and recover from the event without significant disruption to the business. Remember, it may be best to focus on minimizing the effect instead of eliminating the event.

In keeping with the theme of this chapter, time-sensitive events, Table 5-9 is provided to facilitate the thought process and aid in the development of your time-sensitive inventory of events. Remember that you have to look at the complete network in which your organization operates. Once you identify the

Time-Sensitive Event	Prevention Measures	Proactive Action Steps
Humanitarian assistance	Prepare guidelines for actions to be taken in an event to facilitate the notification of next of kin Negotiate lodging, travel, and other arrangements with vendors and suppliers of these services Contract employee assistance providers for on call services as necessary	Assign responsibility Assess costs Prepare purchase and service orders Prepare personnel lists Document for planning purposes

Table 5–8 How to Best Minimize the Impact of a Time-Sensitive Event

particulars of the network, you can begin to define the touchpoints for your organization and the potential time-sensitive events that you will need to address in your business continuity plan.

Time-Sensitive Issues for Analysis	What Makes This a Time-Sensitive Issue?
Financial issues	
Vendor/supplier	
Business applications	
Human resources and staffing	
Legal	
Oversight/documentation	
Transition to recovery organization	
Recovery operations	
Humanitarian assistance	
Infrastructure restoration	
Information recovery and synchronization	
Information and operations synchronization	
Resumption of critical business functions	
Full function restoration	
Permanent restoration	

Table 5–9 Facilitating a Time-Sensitive Event Inventory

Concluding Thoughts

We have discussed time-sensitive events and how you may wish to assess and analyze their potential effects on your organization.

When looking at time-sensitive events, you need to take into account (as you did with "time-critical" events) strategy, competitive intelligence initiatives, and event management as related to how your organization will address these issues.

Included were examples of how to assess time-sensitive events and some time-sensitive events that your organization may wish to consider as starting points for assessment and analysis. As with previous chapters, this is intended to build upon your assessment capabilities.

You should be able to apply these concepts to develop a listing of time-sensitive events that would have potential impacts at all levels within your organization and its value chain.

References

Caponigro, Jeffrey, R., *The Crisis Counselor*, 1998

Sikich, Geary W., "Business Continuity in Times of Uncertainty: Building Pyramids, Cathedrals or Sandcastles," *Disaster Recovery Journal* Fall Conference, September 2002

Chapter Six

THE HIBERNATING "CRISIS:" TIME-DEPENDENT ISSUES

Chapter Summary

In this chapter, we will discuss *time-dependent issues*—issues often overlooked during a "crisis" situation.

Like their predecessors—time-critical and time-sensitive issues—time-dependent issues can cause a "crisis" for your enterprise. They are also the issues having the most long-term impacts on your enterprise. Included in this chapter are examples of time-dependent issues that can affect your enterprise. These issues include, but are not limited to:

- government relations
- corporate relations
- corporate image
- banking and finance
- assigned relocation sites

DEFINITION OF TERMS USED IN THIS CHAPTER

Time-dependent
Time frame of reference for determining crisis

Classification system
Trigger points for activation of plan

- communication systems requirements
- operations systems requirements
- personnel requirements
- documentation of facilities recovery
- assessment of operations requirements
- documents/records required in an emergency
- public sector contacts
- forms and supplies
- associated plans and information
- insurance and risk management plan
- treasury contingency cash plan
- controller's system for tracking recovery expenses
- vendor/supplier/consultant list
- floor space alternatives outside main office
- records planning, storage, and retrieval

This chapter is intended to help you to identify loss, assess the consequences of loss, and provide a basis for mitigation planning should an event occur where you have to address one or more of the time-dependent issues discussed. The outcome you should achieve is a concept for the structure and application of your business continuity management plan for addressing the consequences of time-dependent issues at various levels of your organization.

Time-dependent. The loss or degradation of any business function, related value chain component, internal and/or external infrastructures, the result of which loss or degradation poses a long-term threat to the survival of the enterprise.

Classification system. A system for determining the severity of an event utilizing a unique set of criteria to define and measure the level of severity of the event.

Introduction

In the previous chapters, I introduced the concepts of *time-critical* and *time-sensitive*. In this chapter, I continue to address "time issues." For our purposes we will define *time-dependent* as:

> *The loss or degradation of any business function, related value chain component, internal and/or external infrastructures, such that the result of that loss or degradation poses a long-term threat to the survival of the enterprise.*

The chapter overview provided a list of potential time-dependent areas. We will discuss each and expand on the tools for analysis that were presented in the previous chapters. You should now be able to use these tools to determine time-dependent issues for your organization.

Time-Dependent Events

Previously, I asked you to take a survey determining how well prepared you and your organization are to respond to, manage, and recover from time-critical and time-sensitive events. In this chapter, we will take the same survey, only this time we will focus on time-dependent events (Table 6-1).

	Yes	No
Is your organization prepared to respond to, manage, and recover from a time-dependent event?		
Has your organization ever experienced a time-dependent event?		
Do you think it might someday experience a time-dependent event?		
Have you ever played a part in managing an event (crisis)?		
Have you participated in managing a crisis that you thought could have been handled more effectively with greater preparation?		
Are you concerned that your organization is vulnerable to a time-dependent event?		
Are your instincts telling you that something should be done now to help your organization prevent events from occurring or escalating in severity?		
Are you sometimes confused by the advice you read or are given on event management?		
Do you have the authority to take action to implement an event management program within your organization?		

Evaluation:

0–3 "Yes" answers—Your business is more fortunate than most or you might be underestimating the potential for an event in your business
4–6 "Yes" answers—Your business is vulnerable to an event.
If it hasn't occurred already, you're quite fortunate
6–8 "Yes" answers—You've probably lived through one or more crises, or will experience an event soon. You are likely in a business extremely vulnerable to events that can easily turn into a crisis

Table 6–1 Time-Dependent survey

Based on the results of your answers in the previous two chapters, coupled with your answers here, you should have established a very good understanding concerning your organization's ability to respond to, manage, and recover from time-critical, time-sensitive, and time-dependent events.

The next step, as in the previous chapters, is to identify time-dependent events for your organization. Once you have a list of time-dependent events, you can begin to analyze them to determine the common effects these events would trigger. Using the LMSCARVER™ analysis tool with modifications to fit your organization, you should determine effective strategies for identifying and addressing time-dependent event response, management, mitigation, and recovery operations.

TIME-DEPENDENT—EFFECTS ON BUSINESS CONTINUITY

Take the quiz I introduced in the previous chapters, but this time answer the questions in relation to "time-dependent" events (Table 6-2). As before, in order to get full point values for a question, you must answer the entire question "yes." As a reminder, there are several questions asking for answers to specific sub-elements. If you answer "no" to any one of the sub-elements, you should score the entire question as having been answered "no."

Questions 3 and 4 have been modified to relate to the topics from the previous chapters. You may wish to consider reviewing your answers to these questions once you have completed reading this chapter. Forms from the previous chapters will be used to further the analysis process.

#		Yes	No
1	Have written standards for management performance been established?		
2	Has your organization identified time-critical functions, that if disrupted for 0-3 days could create a crisis? (If you answer no, read the chapter on time-critical again!)?		
3	Has your organization identified time-sensitive functions, that if disrupted for 4-7 days could create a crisis? (If you answer no, you did not read the last chapter!)?		
4	Has your organization identified its time-dependent functions, that if disrupted for 8+ days could create a crisis?		
5	Does your organization depend on external resources to support business functions?		
6	Could the loss of a core business function cascade throughout your organization?		
7	Does your organization have adequate funds in reserve or access to capital resources to operate for a period of 30 days?		
8	Has a specific business continuity management plan (BCMP) been developed for each business process?		
9	Does the BCMP address the loss of the following critical infrastructures/services:		
	Telecommunications and information systems		
	Utilities (electric, gas, water)		
	Energy sources/supply		
	Financial and capital resources		
	Vital human resources and services		
	Transportation services		
	Value chain services and resources (suppliers, customers, etc.)		
	External services and resources (medical, government, etc.)		
10	Is the BCMP integrated, cross-referenced, and indexed?		
11	Does the BCMP address the following six critical functions:		
	Management decision making		
	Planning (tactical, strategic, competitive intelligence)		
	Operations (time-critical, time-sensitive, time-dependent)		
	Logistics (near-term, long-term, vendors, suppliers)		
	Finance (capital on-hand, capital for 30 days operations)		
	Administration (critical human resources and services)		
12	Is there a single point of authority for the coordination of the BCMP?		
13	Has your organization conducted simulations (drills) to validate the BCMP?		
14	Are all commitments made in the BCMP:		
	Identified		
	Documented		
	Verified		
15	Does the BCMP address the following steps and establish time frames in the response/recovery process for:		
	initial response strategies, including classification of incident		
	activation of alternate strategies and sites		
	restoration of critical processes		
	infrastructure restoration		
	information recovery and synchronization		
	full function restoration		
	permanent restoration		

Table 6–2 Business Continuity Quiz—Time-dependent Issues

Once you have completed the quiz, tally your answers and the points generated on the form below (Table 6-3). The goal is an honest representation of your organization's business continuity capabilities.

Question #	Point Value	Yes	No
1	6		
2	6		
3 .	6		
4	6		
5	6		
6	6		
7	6		
8	6		
9	10		
10	6		
11	9		
12	6		
13	6		
14	6		
15	9		
Total	100		

Table 6–3 Scoring

Compare your answers with the scores you had when you took the quiz in the last two chapters. How do your answers regarding time-dependent issues vary from your answers for time-critical and time-sensitive issues?

As you did in the previous chapters, create a table identifying the issue, resources required, and responsible party. I recommend that you complete this useful exercise for time-dependent issues as you did for time-critical and time-sensitive issues. The results should provide you further direction for the development of business continuity within your organization.

Once you have completed the table, your organization can begin to assess the time-dependent aspects of events.

Table 6-4 (as provided in previous chapters) is an example of events that could occur to any organization. Complete this table by determining the time-dependent consequences and effects that would result from the occurrence of an event. As with time-critical and time-sensitive events, I use a series of time frames to determine time-dependent consequences and effects for clients. As cited in previous chapters, these time frames will vary from organization to organization and perhaps within the organization.

Event	Probability (H,M,L)			Impact (H,M,L)			Time - Dependent Consequences	Effect: "Crisis" Trigger Point
Financial issues								
Vendor/supplier								
Business applications								
Human resources and staffing								
Legal								
Oversight/documentation								
Transition to recovery organization								
Recovery operations								
Humanitarian assistance								
Infrastructure restoration								
Information recovery and synchronization								
Information and operations synchronization								
Resumption of critical business functions								
Full function restoration								
Permanent restoration								
Other: describe any event not listed above								

Table 6–4 Events That Could Occur to Any Organization

Once you have completed this assessment, you should have a pretty good idea of the time-dependent parameters (time from occurrence to "crisis") for your organization. As with time-critical and time-sensitive events, your next step is to categorize the time-dependent events into manageable clusters.

Using the LMSCARVER™ principles, refine your assessment of time-dependent events. Develop a series of tables describing time-dependent events for your organization as depicted in Table 6-5.

Highly likely to occur:	
1.	
2.	
3.	
4.	
5.	
Could occur, but unlikely in the near term:	
1.	
2.	
3.	
4.	
5.	
Is Unlikely to occur:	
1.	
2.	
3.	
4.	
5.	

Table 6-5 Possible Time-Dependent Situations—Probability of Occurrence

Once you have completed the initial listing of possible time-dependent events based on probability of occurrence, you need to assess the impact on your business operations. Take the lists and work them into Table 6-6.

Would have serious impact:	
1.	
2.	
3.	
4.	
5.	
Would have impact, but could be managed:	
1.	
2.	
3.	
4.	
5.	
Would have little impact and could be managed easily:	
1.	
2.	
3.	
4.	
5.	

Table 6–6 Possible Time-Dependent Situations—Impact on the Business

Now that you have established a rank ordering of the time-dependent events that could occur and ranked them by impact on the business, you can further assess them against Table 6-7. The goal is to identify and define time-dependent events of the highest priority and that will require the most resources to address from a planning, response, management, and recovery perspective.

Highly likely to occur/would have serious impact:	
1.	
2.	
3.	
4.	
5.	
Highly likely to occur/would have impact, but could be managed:	
1.	
2.	
3.	
4.	
5.	
Could occur, but unlikely in the near term/would have serious impact:	
1.	
2.	
3.	
4.	
5.	

Table 6–7 Highest Priority Time-Dependent Situations—Most Likely and Greatest Impact

Once you have completed the three-part process using the LMSCARVER™ principles, you will have narrowed your list of time-dependent events down based on probability of occurrence and impact to the business. With this information, you can begin to develop some proactive measures addressing the time-dependent events that could put your organization into a crisis, disrupt business continuity, and potentially threaten survival of the organization.

As previously, complete Table 6-8 for each of the time-dependent events that you have identified. The goal is to determine how to best minimize the impact of a time-dependent event so that your organization can effectively respond to, manage, and recover from the event without significant disruption to the business. Remember, it may be best to focus on minimizing the effect instead of eliminating the event.

In keeping with the theme of this chapter, Table 6-9 facilitates the thought process and aids in the development of your "time-dependent" inventory of events. Remember, you have to look at the complete network in which your organization operates. Once you identify the particulars of the network, you can

Time-Dependent Event	Prevention Measures	Proactive Action Steps
Documents/records required in an emergency	Prepare listing of documents/records required in an emergency Create duplicate documents/records and arrange for alternate storage location Maintain lists current and replace outdated documents as necessary Periodically evaluate alternate storage location for security, accessibility, and adequacy	Assign responsibility Assess costs Prepare documents/records lists and duplicates Contract for alternative storage space Document for planning purposes

Table 6–8 How Best to Minimize the Effects of a Time-Dependent Event

begin to define the touchpoints for your organization and the potential time-dependent events you will need to address in your business continuity plan.

Time-Dependent Issues for Analysis	What Makes This a "Time-Dependent" Issue?
Government relations	
Corporate relations	
Corporate image	
Banking and finance	
Assigned relocation sites	
Communication systems requirements	
Operations systems requirements	
Personnel requirements	
Documentation of facilities recovery	
Assessment of operations requirements	
Documents/records required in an emergency	
Public sector contacts	
Forms and supplies	
Associated plans and information	
Insurance and risk management plan	
Treasury contingency cash plan	
Controller's system for tracking recovery expenses	
Vendor, supplier, consultant list	
Floor space alternatives outside main office	
Records planning, storage, and retrieval	

Table 6–9 Facilitating a Time-Dependent Event Inventory

Concluding Thoughts

We have discussed "time-dependent" events and how you may wish to assess and analyze their potential effects on your organization.

When looking at time-dependent events, you need to take into account—as you did with time-critical and time-sensitive events—strategy, competitive intelligence initiatives, and event management relating to how your organization will address these issues.

Included were examples of how to assess time-dependent events and some time-dependent events that your organization may wish to consider as starting points for assessment and analysis. As with previous chapters, this is intended to build upon your assessment capabilities.

By completing these tasks, you should be able to apply these concepts to develop a listing of time-dependent events that would have potential impacts at all levels within your organization and its value chain.

References

Caponigro, Jeffrey, R. *The Crisis Counselor*, 1998

Sikich, Geary W., "Business Continuity in Times of Uncertainty: Building Pyramids, Cathedrals or Sandcastles," *Disaster Recovery Journal* Fall Conference, September 2002

Chapter Seven

Business Continuity: From Inception to Integration

Chapter Summary

In this chapter, we will discuss the business continuity management cycle. This discussion will offer an approach that ties together the elements of your organization's business continuity management plans. Included are examples of a business continuity management plan with a brief description of the sections that should apply to all levels of your enterprise. These include, but are not limited to:

- strategy
- competitive intelligence
- event response, management, recovery
- public, investor, media relations
- maintaining preparedness

DEFINITION OF TERMS USED IN THIS CHAPTER

Classification system
Trigger points for activation of plan

This chapter is intended to help you organize the elements for a business continuity plan for your enterprise.

The outcome you should achieve is a working knowledge of the components of a business continuity plan that can be implemented throughout your organization and exported to external entities—a plan that ensures continuity, ease of understanding, and enhanced communications internally and externally.

Classification system. A system for determining the severity of an event utilizing a unique set of criteria to define and measure the level of severity of the event. The classification system should be designed to facilitate the monitoring and reporting of events impacting the organization's business continuity.

Introduction

In the previous chapters, I introduced concepts for assessment and analysis. Those tools should enable you to develop a robust program for assessment of time-critical, time-sensitive, and time-dependent issues. Here, I am going to discuss an approach to developing a business continuity system for your organization.

Chapter 1 defined the concept of business continuity. I restate it here in order to clarify its components.

All initiatives taken to assure the survival, growth, and resilience of the enterprise.

In the overview, I provided a list of potential topics for discussion. We will discuss each and relate them to the assessment tools that were presented in previous chapters. This combination of assessment and planning tools should provide sufficient resources to begin the process of addressing the definition provided.

In chapters 1-6, I presented methodologies for analysis and determination of what is "at risk" and what the potential impact of a disruption would be. This process can be subdivided into six distinct steps. Each step builds on previous steps (Table 7-1).

Vulnerability, threat, hazard and risk, consequence, assessment and analysis	Assess existing strategy competitive intelligence initiatives and event mitigation programs	Determine critical processes (core business) strategy, competitive intelligence relationships	Develop ranking criteria (time-critical, time-sensitive, time-dependent)	Determine impacts (worst case, best case, most probable case scenarios) on strategy, competitive intelligence, and event management	Develop management response and recovery objectives (MRRO)

Table 7–1 Phase I: Assessment and Impact Analysis

I have presented tools that I have found useful for the initial step in the process—assessment of vulnerability, threat, hazard, risk, and consequence, and analysis. Now let us turn our attention to the next phase: strategy selection.

Business Continuity Strategy Selection

Strategy selection is the process of determining what your organization's capabilities are and what your organization is willing to commit itself to in order to ensure its business continuity. Your selection should take into account the variables of strategy—mission, vision, values—and competitive intelligence initiatives (on the internal side) and on the value-chain relationships your organization maintains (on the external side).

Table 7-2 is a simplified depiction of the process of strategy selection.

Define event management, response, recovery strategy alternatives	Compare alternatives to required time frames and resources	Perform cost benefit analysis for each alternative	Determine response, recovery time frames, and resources required	Establish preferred strategy	Document strategy selection rationale

Table 7–2 Phase II: Strategy Evaluation and Selection

Each of these steps in the selection process should be assessed against strategy and competitive intelligence initiatives. By the time you are ready to document your strategy selection, you should have an integrated picture of your organization's capabilities regarding its ability to fulfill the commitments under the strategy selected.

It is very important to understand the commitments your organization makes in the area of business continuity. Some of the commitments may be driven by regulations that must be complied with; others may be the result of your organization's overall strategy—mission, vision, values—while still others are going to result from your organization's desire to retain a competitive edge in its marketplace.

Another consideration is the value chain proposition mentioned in previous chapters. When embarking on a strategy selection, it will be beneficial to consider the value chain as you develop your preferred strategy. Simply stated: The more integrated your value chain, the more you need to include it, early on, in the business continuity planning process. This is especially true if any one of your value chain components is critical to your organization's survival. This is where time-critical, time-sensitive, and time-dependent analysis comes in handy. This is also an area where you can involve the value chain components in the planning process.

An example of business continuity strategy follows: The mission statement from a plan developed for a client in the financial services industry.

Business Continuity Philosophy: XYZ Company

XYZ Company's business continuity philosophy is based on our business strategy, competitive intelligence initiatives, and our event management capabilities.

XYZ Company's event management philosophy is based on three precepts: Prevention, Preparedness, and Proactive Response.

Effective response and management of events are essential to XYZ Company's business philosophy, because we want to minimize the impact of any event on shareholder value. We are committed to this goal through a proactive event management effort focused on protecting our people, operations, and assets.

Response to events affecting XYZ Company operations will be coordinated by an Event Management Team supported by Consequence Management Plans, Staff, and Technology applications. We will comply with applicable laws and regulations in the implementation of our event response, management, and effort.

Name _____

Title _____

Once you select a strategy, the next step is to begin the plan documentation process.

Business Continuity Plan: A Living Document

The business continuity plan—a living document? This is a concept that, while easy to express, seems very difficult for many to comprehend. Most planning is accomplished with the publication of a written document (or, in this age of information, on a diskette, CD, or interactive plan on the computer). The reality is, however, that, once documented, the plan requires constant care and nurturing. Part of my rationale for redefining business continuity is the result of learning this lesson too many times. In the course of my consulting career, I have had the opportunity to create business continuity, crisis management, emergency response, and disaster recovery plans for a wide spectrum of industries and service organizations. One thing that stands out clearly in my mind is that these plans generally do not stay current very long.

Part of the difficulty in keeping plans current is the amount of information in them. Another reason, and one that I feel is primary, is that no one wants to retain ownership once the plan has been developed; if they do take ownership, the plan maintenance cycle is not adequately addressed.

Of course, change is another factor in the degradation of many plans. We live in a world of *constant* change! The business community is seemingly in a continual state of flux. Just look at your organization and its value chain. Is it the same as it was a year ago? Is it the same as it was six months ago?

In reading the above, you may feel like throwing in the towel and forgetting about developing a business continuity plan for your organization. That would be wrong. The plan should be developed as a *guidance* document, reflecting your organization's strategy commitments, its competitive intelligence initiatives, and its capabilities to identify, assess, classify, respond to, manage, and recover from events. This is critical to the success of the organization. A well thought-out and documented business continuity plan can be invaluable to an organization.

The process, depicted in Table 7-3, is pretty straightforward. The tricky part is getting all the components to work together and bring down the "silos" that many organizations have a tendency to create. Once this is accomplished, a truly integrated plan—one that reflects the organization's strategy, competitive intelligence initiatives, event management capabilities, and value chain components—can be developed.

I have found that plans are generally poorly integrated within organizations. They are also not reflective of strategy and competitive intelligence initiatives;

Analyze existing policies, plans, procedures, and regulatory requirements	Prepare draft, Event Management, Response, Recovery plan	Prepare draft plan implementing procedures	Review and compile implementing procedures into the plan	Finalize Event Management, Response, Recovery plan and supporting materials	Identify plan commitments and establish tracking system

Table 7–3 Phase III: Plan Development and Documentation

and they surely do not reflect the value chain components adequately. Generally, plans tell one how to respond; the only problem with that is that most event response is dictated by the event and is not driven by the plan as it is written. Simplified points in Table 7-4 are made to highlight the need for truly integrated planning.

Response Planning	Management Planning	Recovery Planning
Near real-time	Broad based	Event specific
Events driven	Issues driven	Capabilities driven
Results oriented	Results oriented	Results oriented
Based on business continuity plan	Based on response actions	Based on management actions (strategy and competitive intelligence initiatives redefined)

Table 7–4 The Need for Integrated Planning

By differentiating response, management, and recovery into three categories, it should be clear that these are very interdependent processes. All three are results oriented. Two are based on previous actions, and one is based on a business continuity plan that, when activated, will serve as a basis for the subsequent actions taken.

It should also be noted that the three areas (response, management, recovery) also need to be segmented horizontally, but integrated vertically. The simplified table below provides an example (Table 7-5).

Level	Expectations	Agenda	Focus
Corporate level	Accurate and timely information	Assessment of strategy and competitive intelligence implications Communicating to stakeholders and value chain Revision and/or amendment of strategy, competitive intelligence initiatives	Stakeholders, value chain, affected and unaffected business units
Business unit	Support from corporate Support to affected element Accurate and timely information	Resources to affected element Prevention of cascade of event to other elements	Affected and unaffected operations Value chain as directly affected
Event location	Support from business unit	Fix the problem	Affected operations

Table 7-5 Response, Management, and Recovery Segmentation

You should develop a similar table for your organization to assist you in differentiating responsibilities at various levels within the organization, integrating planning, providing seamless vertical and horizontal communications, ensuring a common terminology, and addressing value chain and external interfaces (i.e., government entities). You should also begin to ponder those nasty infrastructure issues as you contemplate this simple table.

One problem I often have experienced is that everyone wants to "do something" to mitigate a problem. Often times, this can complicate the response effort. As an energy company client operating at a field location once told a vice-chairman as they conversed telephonically during an exercise, "Don't tell me where to put my boom and I won't tell you how to run the rest of the company!" (The message, by the way, got through to the vice-chairman. He looked over to me and chuckled, "I guess I better focus my attention on issues that I can respond to and not on things I cannot control.")

My point here is that each level involved in assuring the business continuity of the organization has a role to play and an agenda to address. By having a plan in place that fosters understanding and facilitates communication, the expectations, agenda, and *focus* at each level can be addressed without panic, chaos, and confusion.

I offer a similar table as an example for the public sector (Table 7-6). Please note that the public sector can become quite complex with the roles of different agencies and authorities sometimes appearing to conflict.

Level	Expectations	Agenda	Focus
Federal level	Accurate and timely information Support to state and local government	Assessment of national security implications Communicating to general public Declaration of state of emergency and/or disaster	Protection of public International relations National security
State level	Support from federal level Support to local level Accurate and timely information from local level	Protect the public Maintain civil authority	Support to local level, coordination with federal level, and protection of public and infrastructure
Local level	Support from state, and federal entities	Protect the public	Maintain civil authority

Table 7–6 Response, Management, and Recovery for the Public Sector

I think it is extremely important for business and government to develop an understanding of the expectations, agenda, and focus matrix of the other. Table 7-7 presents a very simplified view. You will note that the expectations, agenda, and focus columns vary greatly from business to government.

Level	Business	Government
Expectations	Return to normal operations as quickly as possible	Complete cooperation with civil authorities
Agenda	Fix problem	Protect public, determine the cause of the event, and ensure security interests
Focus	Fix problem, return to business as usual—make profits, meet stakeholder expectations	Protect public, maintain civil authority, and ensure national security interests are met

Table 7-7 Response, Management, and Recovery: Business and Government Mix

This is a key variable that business continuity plans have not addressed well—if at all—to date. As a result of terrorist acts and the threat of terrorism, business is faced with the need to understand that the government's expectations, agenda, and focus are different.

Today, if an event occurs, the likelihood that it will be investigated for possible terrorist involvement should not go unrecognized by business. If a "crime scene" is declared as a result of the investigation, business needs to understand that even though the event has been mitigated, you may not be returning to "business as usual." As such, business continuity planning—incorporating strategy, competitive intelligence initiatives, event management, and value chain considerations—is necessary. We must rethink the concept of business continuity to reflect the current state of world affairs.

I will discuss specific planning elements for consideration in later sections of this chapter and in later chapters of this book.

VALIDATING BUSINESS CONTINUITY PLANS

Once the plan is developed—and, hopefully, before the first scheduled review and revision—you need to address the plan's *validation*. This is a process of communicating, educating, and "seeing what works" under various scenarios. Some would use the term "test" to describe the last part of the validation process, but I choose to use the term "validate" (or "scenario-based verification"). *Test* suggests a "pass/fail" situation. What happens if you fail the test? Does that mean the business continuity plan (and, by implication, strategy, competitive intelligence initiatives, and event management) is worthless? Not worth the paper (or CD, diskette, or drive space) that it is written on? Of course not; it means that in the particular instance, based on scenario inputs, the business continuity plan did not work as anticipated. I can (as can you) devise scenarios that will fail any and all business continuity plans. The goal should be to assess how well the plan (and therefore the system) works under various scenario settings. In this way, you can be constantly vigilant for those events that will put maximum stress on continuity.

As depicted in Table 7-8, the validation and maintenance of business continuity consists of several elements.

Design, develop, and implement Event Management, Response, and Recovery plan training	Design and document plan validation (Simulation) procedures	Develop and facilitate plan validation program	Design and document plan maintenance procedures	Establish plan audit and maintenance schedules	Finalize plan documents and commitment tracking system

Table 7–8 Phase IV: Plan Validation and Maintenance

A key element in assuring business continuity (and one of the most over-looked, under-addressed, and least-appreciated areas) is training. In order for business continuity to work smoothly, training must be developed and implemented. The training program is necessary, if not essential. A staff that does not know the elements of its business continuity plan should not be expected to implement strategy, competitive intelligence initiatives, or respond to, manage, and recover from an event. You would never think of developing strategy and not communicating it to your organization, would you? The same holds true for business continuity. You must communicate knowledge to all personnel with a role in the assurance of business continuity. This means that you must develop and implement training designed to address strategy, competitive intelligence, event management, and the value chain components. As such, your training should address the critical infrastructures upon which your organization is dependent on and the interface aspects with various public sector entities.

Before you train and conduct simulations to determine the effectiveness of the business continuity effort, you need to identify all commitments you have made in the planning documents and associated credentials. I recommend that clients establish commitment identification and tracking systems early in the development of the business continuity plan. This is important to ensure that regulatory-driven commitments are addressed and to ensure that commitments not specified in regulations are identified and addressed. I have seen too many instances in which where an organization has made commitments without realizing what they were committing to.

Elements of the Business Continuity Plan

STRATEGY

I provide here an example of a business continuity strategy in the form of a mission statement from a plan developed for a client in the financial services industry. I think it is important to break down the component parts in order to fully understand business continuity philosophy and the integration of its three component parts—strategy, competitive intelligence, and event management. Below is the example statement.

BUSINESS CONTINUITY PHILOSOPHY: XYZ COMPANY

XYZ Company business continuity philosophy is based on our business strategy, competitive intelligence initiatives, and our event management capabilities. XYZ Company's event management philosophy is based on three precepts: Prevention, Preparedness, and Proactive Response. Effective response and management of events are essential to XYZ Company's business philosophy, because we want to minimize the impact of any event on shareholder value. We are committed to this goal through a proactive event management effort focused on protecting our people, operations, and assets.

Response to events affecting XYZ Company operations will be coordinated by an Event Management Team supported by Consequence Management Plans, Staff, and Technology applications. We will comply with applicable laws and regulations in the implementation of our event response, management, and effort.

Name _____

Title _____

What are the strategy implications for this statement? Well—there are many! But I am not going to delve into a long discussion on strategy because there are far too many good books addressing how to develop it. Let's instead break it down to strategy's three components—mission, vision, and values.

If we look at the statement and assess it against the company's mission statement, we would find that this *business continuity philosophy* embraces the company's *mission statement*—as it should.. The company mission statement is summarized as follows:

Our mission is to deliver world-class asset management services

In order to fulfill its mission statement, the firm is committed to assuring that its clients are able to access the services offered by the company on a 24-hour day, 7 days a week, 52 weeks a year basis. That means that the company, which operates globally, must be able to assure its clients accessibility and provision of services offered—*constantly*.

Let's turn to the second component of strategy—vision. In order to fulfill its mission statement, we can see that the company has made a significant commitment. Vision is the realization of these commitments. Vision is the intangible that drives the organization to achieve its mission. For example, the vision statement for Logical Management Systems, Corp., my consulting practice, reads as follows:

We accomplish our mission by offering our clients the ability to secure their needs through the convenience of a single source consumer service menu.

In order to fulfill the vision statement, we have to offer our clients (and prospective clients) services in keeping with their needs. This, however, can be an arduous task if you try to be everything to everyone. You need to *focus* your vision by understanding the scope of your mission statement and identifying the commitments within the statement so that you can fulfill your organization's vision.

The final component of strategy—values. Defining corporate values is imperative for any organization in today's world. Values drive the mission and vision propositions of strategy. Values are also easily corrupted if not carefully monitored! Values are composed of—

- corporate image
- business ethics
- business practices
- people.

People are the variable in the value component of strategy. We have recently seen so many problems surface—Enron, Anderson, WorldCom, Tyco, and Global Crossing, to name a few. The organizations all had a strategy that consisted of mission, vision, and value statements; the unfortunate fact is that people—people responsible for the ethical operation of these companies—failed to live up to the mission, vision, and value components and as a result, the companies suffered. Business continuity, survival, resilience, and growth ended in the destruction of the companies and their failure to be able to manage events. Could these companies have done things to prepare, prevent, and take proactive action? The obvious answer is, yes.

COMPETITIVE INTELLIGENCE

We have seen that, in order for business continuity to succeed, it must embrace strategy as a component. A second component is competitive intelligence. By competitive intelligence, I mean all that the efforts of your organization makes to secure a competitive advantage in its markets. Competitive intelligence may beget, for some, visions of James Bond, the KGB, CIA, and other clandestine activities. Competitive intelligence is not what it is perceived to be. The Society of Competitive Intelligence Professionals (SCIP) defines competitive intelligence as:

A systematic and ethical program for gathering, analyzing, and managing external information that can affect your company's plans, decisions, and operations.

I would add to this definition that competitive intelligence is also a systematic and ethical means for denying your competitors information that may cause your company to lose competitive advantage in its markets. Competitive intelligence should not be an expensive patchwork of informal networks. Decision-makers cannot afford to be paralyzed by the muddle. Data culled from a mishmash of sources, replete with charts, tables, and spreadsheets can be overwhelming.

Competitive intelligence can be broken down into the following components. Please note that this is a very simplified breakdown. My intention is not to go on with a lengthy discussion of competitive intelligence; there are plenty of books that can provide much valuable information on this subject.

- Acquisition of knowledge
- Analysis of knowledge
- Application of knowledge
- Denial of knowledge
- Misinformation activities
- Data mining
- Human factors

Competitive intelligence enables people to make informed decisions. Making informed decisions leads, generally, to success in execution of business strategies. Competitive intelligence is a continuous process. Competitive intelligence initiatives serve as a basis for strategy development, execution, and management. Competitive intelligence initiatives serve as a basis for event management (response, management, and recovery) activities.

EVENT RESPONSE, MANAGEMENT, RECOVERY

The third component of business continuity as I am defining it is event management. Event management consists of three primary elements:

- Response
- Management
- Recovery

When we analyze these three elements, we find a myriad of sub-elements. The response element consists of detection, classification, initial response, sustained response, and event mitigation. These can be very complex depending on the organization. We have seen in previous chapters how to conduct an assessment of potential issues that may cause a "crisis" for your organization. Now, put those skills into practice and think about what you need to do to detect an imminent event. Detection is a difficult process; however, by linking competitive intelligence initiatives to event management, one can see that a potential source of detection information can be achieved. This can be crucial to an organization. What would change if we could detect, early on, information that would give us an opportunity to prevent an event from occurring, or to minimize the effects from the event in a timely manner? I generally use six criteria for establishing a system of detection for organizations:

- life safety—who is in jeopardy?
- infrastructure—internal and external exposures?
- operational status—what's broken; what's working?
- facility occupancy—can business continue from this location?
- corporate impact—what is our brand image?
- actions underway—who is doing what?

You can add to the above criteria depending on your particular situation. I have developed systems that included environmental considerations, weather conditions, geographic area/location, the commodity involved, and quantity, volume, and toxicity considerations. One of my clients in the energy industry developed the following criteria:

- personnel injury or illness
- damage to property, equipment, or facilities owned, leased, or contracted by the company
- damage to third-party property
- environmental damage
- disruption to the public
- threats to personnel security
- government agency action against the company and/or adverse news media coverage

Once you have a detection system in place you need to develop criteria to assist you in determining the potential severity of an event for your organization.

The value of having a system in place, to classify the potential severity of an event is that your organization can bring to bear all the resources available to respond and mitigate the event in the most timely manner possible, thereby lessening the impact of an event on strategy and competitive intelligence initiatives. Table 7-9 is an example of a detection/classification system.

		Life Safety	Infrastructure	Operational Status	Facility Occupancy	Corporate Impact	Actions in Progress
LOWEST	1	No life threatening injuries No protective actions recommended No employee impact	No loss of critical infrastructure No immediate or long-term impacts	Damage not requiring suspension of operations	No evacuation Facility has no damage	No threat to workforce No threat to company Some liability concerns Media coverage local, limited, or none	Managed locally Advise business continuity management team (BCMT) of situation after situation is controlled
	2	Minor medical injuries Employee welfare impact Protective actions recommended for site and personnel	Loss of critical infrastructure Short-term impact, short duration	Damage requiring short-term or limited suspension of operations, minor impact to time-critical functions and activities	Short to medium duration evacuation Minor facility damage, no relocation of resources	Threat to workforce Threat to company Liability very low Media coverage limited	Managed locally External response limited Limited BCMT activation for advisory purposes Plan partially activated
	3	Serious medical injuries Protective actions recommended for site and nearby areas	Loss of critical infrastructure Near-term impact, medium duration	Significant impact on operations Medium-term suspension of operations, time-critical functions and activities impacted	Medium to long-term evacuation Facility damages requiring relocation of certain resources	Potential for immediate impact on workforce, community, and/or company Medium liability National media coverage	Significant external level response BCMT activated and supporting the response effort Plan fully activated
HIGHEST	4	Loss of life Terrorism Workplace violence Kidnapping Civil disruption Bombing Protective action recommended for site and general public	Loss of critical infrastructure, immediate impact, extended duration	Major impact on operations Long-term loss of operational capability Relocation of time-critical functions and activities	Extended recovery of facility, requiring relocation of workforce for extended time	Immediate impact on employees, community, company Liability high Extensive media coverage Inquiries extensive	Manage at appropriate business level BCMT activated and assisting in securing supplemental external resources, managing business impacts

Table 7–9 Detection/Classification System

Public, investor, media relations (stakeholders)

It used to be that we would say, "We are a media-driven society" to mean the U.S. was the society focused on. Today, like never before, "We are a media-driven *world*." As such, business continuity in the sense that I have defined it is very sensitive and quite reactive to media attention, either positive or negative.

Media attention can quickly change a company's fortunes. This is one of the reasons that I added a column in the classification matrix on corporate impact. As I write this section, today's media attention is focused on corporate America in crisis. It seems that you cannot turn a page in a newspaper or periodical without some report of crisis. The same holds true for the Internet and broadcast media.

Today, more than ever before, effective communication plays an integral role in successful business continuity. The opportunities for communicating are vast. There are approximately 1,150 television stations, 8,200 radio stations, 1,700 daily newspapers, 8,000 weekly newspapers, and more than 12,000 magazines—and the numbers continue to grow!

Management is never put more strongly to the test than in a crisis situation. The objectives are immediate—and so are the results. Management simply must devote sufficient resources to being able to communicate quickly, accurately, and effectively in response to any event, large or small. A routine event can be treated as front-page news by the media. You and your organization must be prepared to deal with public perception, as well as reality. An integral part of your business continuity approach should be to offer guidelines for immediate, effective, and responsive communications. An effective communication program can help resolve an event and maintain your organization's integrity and credibility.

While I will not go into great detail regarding the public, investor, and media relations program, here are some key points to consider:

Speed, connectivity, and intangibles are key drivers. Speed and connectivity give us greater access to information. Greater access to information requires that organization develop knowledge management programs to address the accelerated learning curve that they are faced with. The need for knowledge management programs and the accelerated learning curve combine to force organizations to be more adaptive. Increased adaptability equals a variety of outcomes, unanticipated feedback, potential for cascading effects, and a greater need to maximize assets.

Intangibles are created by execution of strategy, competitive intelligence initiatives, and event management capabilities. Intangibles are a measure of perception and reality. Perception for many is reality. Intangibles are things like corporate image, ethics, and values. When intangibles, speed, and connectivity combine, they can result in success or failure for your organization.

Just take a historical journey through the 1970s to today and you will see how the three elements in Table 7-10 have become major players in business continuity as defined herein.

Event	Perception	Reality
Johnson & Johnson Tylenol poisonings	J&J did a great job and fully recovered their share of the market	J&J did do a great job, because of strong corporate values J&J never fully recovered their share of the market
Exxon Valdez	Largest oil spill ever Untold environmental damage Exxon did a very poor job of responding and cleaning up the spill	The Valdez ranks as the 53rd largest oil spill on record, behind such memorable events as the 68.7 million gallon spill created by the Amoco Cadiz, the 6th largest spill on record Exxon also did a very good job of response and cleanup
Firestone recall	Firestone did not do a good job on the recall of tires	Firestone recalled more than 6 million tires, unfortunately the company delayed the implementation of the recall when it began feuding with Ford over responsibility
Enron debacle	Enron executives really knew what was going on and their accountants collaborated in a cover-up	Lack of checks and balances led to the downfall of the company Executives failed to monitor the business properly
Year 2000 transition	The whole thing was a big hoax	Due to massive efforts to fix and/or patch potentially defective software, and hardware events were minimized Reporting of events that did occur was minimal

Table 7–10 Perception vs. Reality in Business Continuity Planning

A key to a successful public, investor, and media program is knowing who your stakeholders are. *Stakeholders* are people and/or entities that have a vested interest in the success, growth, survivability, and resilience of your organization and—unfortunately—in the possible failure of your organization. A careful assessment of stakeholders is necessary to assure that business continuity is adequately addressed.

MAINTAINING PREPAREDNESS

A final element in the business continuity plan is maintaining preparedness. I addressed training and validation earlier. Maintaining preparedness somewhat encompasses these two areas, but it goes a step further. Maintaining preparedness is the top-down and bottom-up commitment within the organization to execute strategy, competitive intelligence initiatives, and event management in a manner that assures the survival, growth, and resilience of the enterprise.

As you read this, you may be thinking that I have just restated the definition of business continuity provided at the beginning of this book. Well, I did; and the reason for doing it is simple. Unless we are committed to doing the "right thing," organizations, companies, governments, etc. are destined to fail or to perform at such low levels that they will never be as effective as they could be. As a matter of fact, they may, by their lack of performance, be a contributing factor in the cascade of failure that occurs when inadequate attention is given to business continuity.

Concluding Thoughts

We discussed the elements of business continuity. Also presented were concepts for the application of business continuity thinking to your organization and its value chain. We did not get into a cookbook approach to planning because I find each organization must develop solutions unique to the network that they operate in. While I do favor consistency in developing planning materials, I have found that the planning materials must reflect the organization, its strategy, competitive intelligence initiatives, and its ability to fulfill commitments for event response, management, and recovery. Each organization needs to develop a concept of business continuity consistent with how it is structured. Typically, a business model takes the form of three levels—corporate, business unit, and facility, while the government model generally consists of federal, state, local levels. In Table 7-11, I will leave you with my perspective on the key areas for development in respect to event management.

Key Area of Development	Comments
Strategy	Identify mission, vision, and value statements, and that ensure they are reflective of capabilities for business continuity
Competitive intelligence	Establish policy and procedures for securing competitive intelligence information and for denial of information Integrate into event management initiatives
Event management	Develop response, management, and recovery capabilities, and integrate into overall business continuity strategy Ensure resilience of the organization
Decision making	Establish a seamless vertical and horizontal knowledge base for decision making If necessary, develop policy guidance for authority to make decisions on behalf of the organization
Planning	Determine short-term and long-term goals Assess vulnerabilities and determine consequence scenarios Provide planning guidance to the organization
Operations	Integrate all operational elements to remove or reduce silo effects Ensure the integration and synchronization of operations and information management
Logistics	Evaluate value chain issues for the organization Ensure that short-term logistics needs are addressed Ensure that long-term logistics requirements are identified and that alternatives are established
Finance	Provide cost benefit analysis, cost tracking, audit, and other financial services
Administration	Address human resource requirement and issues Serve as documentation repository for the organization
Infrastructure	Identify internal core infrastructures, and develop graceful degradation and agile restoration plan and procedures Identify external infrastructure dependencies, develop alternative resource strategies, and establish coordination with external infrastructure resources
Value chain	Identify stakeholders and integrate them into the business continuity process for your organization Ensure that alternative sources are identified and that relationships are established

Table 7–11 Key Areas in the Development of Event Management

Listed below are key elements of a typical event management plan. These may prove helpful for getting started in the planning process:

- Section 1—Event Response: The initial response activities and subsequent sustained management/response activities
- Section 2—Command Center and Alternate Site Activation: The steps and considerations for activation and operation of the organization's command center and relocation of critical business functions to alternate sites as necessary
- Section 3—Infrastructure Restoration: The process for critical infrastructure (internal/external) identification and restoration oversight by the business continuity management team
- Section 4—Information Systems and Operations Recovery and Synchronization: The process establishes guidelines for the recovery of operations and information systems and synchronization of operations and information systems. Included should be a discussion on reestablishment of information flow critical to value chain operations
- Section 5—Resumption of Critical Business Functions: The process and oversight functions to be performed by the business continuity management team in assuring that critical business functions are reestablished
- Section 6—Full Function Restoration: The activities of the business continuity management team during the recovery phase of operations
- Section 7—Permanent Restoration: The "return to normal" phase of operations by the business continuity management team
- Section 8—Maintaining Preparedness: Training, plan validation (event simulation exercises), plan maintenance, provisions for periodic review, and update of the elements of the business continuity plan (strategy, competitive intelligence initiatives, and event management)
- Appendices: Contain material that is subject to frequent change, such as copies of forms, checklists, and communication directories. This material should be organized to support business continuity while allowing for rapid updating and distribution
- Event Plan Implementing Procedures (EPIP): Contain specific detailed instructions and guidance for all aspects of the event management plan. EPIPs assign responsibilities to personnel and include flowcharts and checklists where appropriate to improve event response, management, and recovery operations

The key plan sections introduce concepts that are expanded upon and supported by appendices; EPIPs, however, are the tools used to implement the plan. They are grouped into four categories. The specific numbers appearing in each series may vary from organization to organization.

Regardless of where the plan is implemented, however, there should be consistent naming conventions and structure of EPIPs for the organization. EPIPs can be categorized as follows:

Administrative. Administrative EPIPs consist of non-event management guidelines. Administrative EPIPs prescribe the manner in which activities such as monthly calibration tests or communications tests are to be accomplished.

Event classification. Event classification procedures provide step-by-step immediate action guidelines for identification and classification of an event.

Event response/management/recovery organization. These procedures provide guidance for personnel who areassigned duties in the event management plan.

Event operations. These procedures provide guidelines for conducting event mitigation operations. They are step-by-step instructions to direct activities during an event.

Re-entry and recovery. These procedures include step-by-step guidance for the recovery and synchronization of operations and information systems to their pre-event status.

EPIP format. EPIPs should be sufficiently detailed to guide personnel actions during an event. Disruptive events may not follow anticipated patterns, so the EPIPs should be written to provide sufficient flexibility to accommodate various situations. The EPIPs should include the following provisions:

- Purpose: This management practice provides guidance and instructions for personnel who are assigned to recovery locations

- Scope: This section lists the individuals, by position description, who generally will implement the EPIP

- References: References to other supporting documents, technical information, and other sources of information are listed in this section

- Definitions: With the paucity of acronyms, abbreviations, and foreshortened wordings, it is advisable to define any new or unusual terminology. This section of the EPIP also clarifies any terms as to their meaning

- Responsibilities: A listing of responsibilities, general information, initial actions, and subsequent actions is provided to assist the individual to implement the EPIP

- Procedure : This section contains information pertinent to the accomplishment of the function or task prescribed in the EPIP
- Flowchart: Any supporting flowcharts, diagrams, or other pictorial representation of steps in the EPIP
- Approval: This section contains the signature blocks and signatures of the approval authorities for the EPIP

References

Davis, Stanley M., Christopher Meyer. *Blur: The Speed of Change in the Connected Economy*

Largest Oil Spills, Oil Spill Intelligence Report, Cutter Information Corp., 2000

Sikich, Geary W. It Can't Happen Here: All Hazards Crisis Management Planning, PennWell Publishing, 1993

———Logical Management Systems, Corp. AUDITRAK^{tm} Diagnostic Assessment Program (www.logicalmanagement.com)

———Logical Management Systems, Corp. (www.logicalmanagement.com), LMSCARVER™ Touchpoint Analysis Diagnostic Program, 2000

———Managing Crisis at the Speed of Light, Disaster Recovery Journal Conference, 1999

———All Hazards Crisis Management Planning, Airport Professional, Issue 8, 1999, The Airport Mobility Network Group

$$\left[\text{Chapter Eight} \right]$$

PROTECTING YOUR ORGANIZATION IN THE AGE OF UNCERTAINTY

Chapter Summary

In this chapter, we discuss ways in which your organization can limit its exposures to potential situations that may develop into a "crisis." This chapter will investigate the value of competitive intelligence collection prior to and during an event. Included are examples of intelligence collection processes, what to do with the information collected, and how to minimize your organization's exposure to crises.

This chapter is intended to help you to identify critical information sources, information flow paths within your organization, information sources from external sources to your organization, and information flow from your organization to external sources. The outcome you should achieve is a concept for defining information needs, developing a collection, analysis, and dissemination methodology for this information, and the use of competitive intelligence for critical decision-makers at various levels of your organization.

DEFINITION OF TERMS USED IN THIS CHAPTER

Competitive intelligence
Time frame of reference for determining crisis

Information
Trigger points for activation of plan

Knowledge management
Management of institutional awareness

Intelligence life cycle
Information processing cycle from raw data to intelligence

Counterintelligence
Efforts to deny competitors information on your business

HUMINT
Human intelligence

Competitive intelligence. Underlying principles and foundations providing focus for the business. Strategy consists of mission, vision, and value statements, and the policies and procedures supporting the organization.

Information. All initiatives to assure the acquisition and/or denial of data, information, and other considerations to gain and retain competitive advantage.

Knowledge management. The identification and management of institutional awareness, expertise, skills, and wisdom to support the enterprise.

Intelligence life cycle. The process of collecting, collating, analyzing, validating, distributing, and controlling data that transformed into intelligence.

Counterintelligence. Operations undertaken to deny information to competitors for the purpose of retaining a competitive edge.

HUMINT. Human intelligence collection efforts.

Introduction

Business agility and *resilience* remain popular buzzwords. Today your organization must be poised to respond immediately to any business condition or value chain request and leap on any new opportunity. This creates yet another set of challenges and responsibilities requiring executives to view business continuity in a whole new light.

Today's executives have three spheres of concern:

- *Sphere of responsibility*—Defined by your corporate strategy (mission, vision, values), competitive intelligence initiatives, and event management capabilities

- *Sphere of influence*—Defined as your assets and capabilities and how they can affect the courses of action of others

- *Sphere of interest*—Defined as how the assets and capabilities of others can affect your courses of action

This chapter introduces concepts addressing how you can protect your organization in an age of uncertainty. The spheres of concern (as defined above) play heavily on the ability to protect the organization. Critical to all three spheres is how your organization collects and uses information, commonly referred to as intelligence. However, for our purposes, we will define *intelligence* as follows:

> *Intelligence is the refined product of information gathering efforts. Intelligence consists of data (information) that can be used to facilitate decision-making through the application of knowledge, such that the result of the decision(s) facilitates business continuity for the enterprise and its value chain.*

In the overview, I said this chapter is intended to help you identify critical information sources, information flow paths within your organization, information sources from external sources to your organization, and information flow from your organization to external sources. Let us now embark upon the journey to intelligence.

Competitive Intelligence

If intelligence is the refined product of information gathering, what exactly are the components of information gathering? The following points provide a brief summary of information gathering and its subsequent transformation into usable intelligence. Please note that my emphasis is on the word "usable" in the previous sentence. Intelligence without a purpose or use is merely noise. Today's business organizations cannot afford to have "noise" cluttering the decision-making process!

The components of intelligence are:

- acquisition of knowledge (information in the form of data)
- analysis of knowledge (data turned into usable intelligence)
- application of knowledge (decision-making based on intelligence)

- denial of knowledge (application of the sphere of influence)
- misinformation activities (creation of noise)
- data mining (collecting, collating, analyzing, validating, distributing, and controlling)
- human factors (the wild card in your business continuity efforts)

In order for your organization to achieve business continuity, as defined herein, the competitive intelligence component cannot be overlooked. I have said it before in this book, but I feel that it bears saying again: *Competitive intelligence provides a basis for strategy and event management.* Your competitive intelligence program must be based on establishing essential elements of analysis (EEA) supported by measures of effectiveness (MOE) and refined through the answering of specific measurable and observable measures of performance (MOP). Competitive intelligence has to take a systematic approach and avoid becoming an expensive patchwork creating more noise than usable intelligence. I coined the following statement to underscore the importance of the competitive intelligence component to business continuity.

Information, no matter how well managed, is not knowledge unless it can be used.

Protecting Your Organization in the Age of Uncertainty

WHY IS COMPETITIVE INTELLIGENCE SO IMPORTANT?

Correct and effective assessments permit decision-makers an opportunity to effectively prioritize strategy and to initiate and sustain event response activities. It allows executives to allocate scarce resources and evaluate the responsiveness of your organization's value chain in a timely manner.

WHO SHOULD COLLECT COMPETITIVE INTELLIGENCE?

The collection of competitive intelligence information and its assessment require a broad-based effort from all elements of the organization. You should consider establishing a clearinghouse function responsible for collating, analyzing, and disseminating the final product to the appropriate decision-makers and users.

When you have answered these questions, you can start to focus on developing strategy and event management initiatives that will protect your organization in times of rapid change and uncertainty. In other words, you can "walk the talk" of business agility and resilience.

Table 8-1 is designed to assess your organization's current level of competitive intelligence vulnerability.

Protecting Your Organization	Yes	No
Are your organization's critical information sources documented?		
Has your organization mapped its information flow paths?		
Is information from external sources to your organization validated?		
Are controls in place to manage information going to external sources?		
Does your organization have a system for defining information needs?		
Is there a clearinghouse function for competitive intelligence information?		
Are competitive intelligence documents distributed to critical decision makers?		
Are competitive intelligence documents distributed to various levels of staff?		
Does your organization conduct background checks on staff?		
Does your organization conduct background checks on key personnel?		
Total		

Table 8-1 Assessing Current Competitive Intelligence Vulnerabilities

For every "yes" answer, award yourself 10 points. For every "no" answer, subtract 10 points. There are a total of 100 points you can get for answering all of the questions "yes." There are a total of minus 100 you can get for answering every question "no." Tally up your score and see how you did.

EVALUATION

0-3 "No" answers—Your organization is more fortunate than most or you might be underestimating the potential for sensitive intelligence information to be leaving your organization

4-6 "No" answers—Your organization is vulnerable to a loss of competitive advantage in its marketplace. If it hasn't occurred already, you're quite fortunate

6-8 "No" answers—You've probably lived through one or more crises, or will experience an event soon. You are likely in an organization that is extremely vulnerable to competitive intelligence initiatives from other organizations

There are many more questions you may wish to ponder in addition to the 10 posited above, e.g., "Does your organization outsource?" You should also recognize that by merely answering "yes" or "no" to the questions, there is no assurance your organization is protected against predators. As a matter of fact, you probably will find the questions lead to more introspection and a need to answer the "how" derivative form of the questions.

Take, for example, the question, "Are your organization's critical information sources documented?" By adding "how" to the start of the question you have to answer in much more detail. Can you comfortably answer the questions in the assessment in that kind of detail? Place the emphasis on the word "comfortably" as you read the revised question.

Think about the following lead-in line from a recent newsletter I received from Global Continuity (www.globalcontinuity.com), a business continuity information clearinghouse. Does your organization fall into this category?

80% OF COMPANIES LACK INFORMATION AVAILABILITY PLANS

A study of 200 companies conducted by an independent research firm for SunGard Availability Services has found that companies of all sizes are remarkably unprepared to keep their key information processing systems running in the event of a system or network disruption.

Source: GlobalContinuity, June 2002 Newsletter

If the above is any indication of how business is addressing a critical aspect of operations, then is it indicative that competitive intelligence information is hemorrhaging from just as many organizations?

10 ACTIONS YOUR ORGANIZATION CAN TAKE NOW

Since the Sept. 11, 2001 terrorist attack on the U.S., the traditional rules governing the conduct of business are being obliterated as businesses begin to redefine how they will operate in an era of uncertainty. The world was well on its way to blurring the distinction between traditional business and the appearance of widespread eBusiness operations, anyway—products were becoming services; services becoming products; and business lines were changing constantly. As the authors of the book *Blur* state:

> *Connectivity, Speed and Intangible Values are the new driving forces in business today. Traditional business boundaries are blurring as everyone becomes electronically connected.*

With all of the emphasis on connectivity, you might ask yourself, "How resilient is my organization if our connectivity is interrupted?" In his book, *6 Nightmares*, Anthony Lake relates the comments of World War II veterans, stating:

> *...that battle was a struggle not just between two opposing armies but between two opposing ideas, and the qualities those ideas engendered in their respective fighting forces.*

With the tragic events of September 11, governments, people, and corporations all over the world entered a new era of thought and belief. No longer are we able to ignore potential vulnerabilities in our intelligence systems (government or business).

We have created global reach via the evolution of transcontinental travel, the Internet, communications media, and worldwide business expansion. Our new global economy requires us to understand how intelligence is used and how intelligence needs to be protected. The challenge for business executives, government leaders, and staff at all levels is to maximize the benefits of near-instantaneous information while maintaining security within ever-changing organizational structures and value chains.

Government and corporate America have long recognized the importance of being prepared. In the wake of many events, government passed regulations requiring corporate America to develop and implement programs to assure preparedness. Implementing the following 10 actions in Table 8-2 for your organization and its value chain can produce positive results. The 10 actions are presented in no order of precedence. You and your organization should assess their applicability and prioritize them as it fits your unique situation.

Action #1	Make your enterprise an unattractive target
Action #2	Revise employee screening processes
Action #3	Validate business, community, and government contacts
Action #4	Assess business continuity plans
Action #5	Train and educate your workforce
Action #6	Equip your workforce
Action #7	Review leases and contracts for risk exposure
Action #8	Assess value-chain exposure to supply disruptions
Action #9	Review insurance policies and conduct cost/benefit analysis
Action #10	Communicate commitment

Table 8–2 10 Actions

ACTION #1—MAKE YOUR ENTERPRISE AN UNATTRACTIVE TARGET

Making your enterprise an unattractive target is one of the basic tenants of security, as well as business continuity. Whether it is a terrorist or a criminal, if your enterprise presents significant barriers to access, it is less likely to be targeted. The application of active security measures, as well as passive security measures, serves to deflect the perpetrator to another target. For example, you may wish to change your security personnel's uniforms in order to make them more visible. A simple change like this can have an effect by making people more aware of the presence of the security personnel. You can introduce "target hardening" measures, such as decorative concrete barriers, cameras, perimeter lighting, and access badges. These measures act as passive deterrents to unauthorized entry. You can also add barriers to access, such as manned guard emplacements with gates, tire spikes, reinforced fencing, and the removal of vegetation next to building parking areas.

You can deny competitive intelligence information to others by introducing greater document and access control measures. Just take a look at your website and/or annual report (if your organization produces one) and see how much information is accessible to the general public. Some organizations choose to put photographs of key personnel on their websites. This can pose a serious risk for those personnel. Kidnapping is a major industry in some countries, and today many executives travel extensively.

ACTION #2—REVISE EMPLOYEE SCREENING PROCESSES

Do you really know who your employees are? Are you sure that the person you hire has represented his/her background honestly? Taking this action may assist you and your organization solve a very real problem, "How do I know?" More than ever, employers need to identify employees and potential employees who are at risk of being exploited, compromised, and/or co-opted by terrorists or criminals for information, access, and/or passive cooperation. The better you know your employees, the less likely your organization presents a target. You can accomplish this through implementing a system of more detailed background investigations designed to provide assurance of the information provided to your organization.

Implementing a system of checks and balances whereby critical information and/or access is not subject to compromise can also afford your organization more security. A "workplace violence" program is also useful for diffusing potential conflict situations. Employee assistance programs should be reviewed and assessed for effectiveness and for accessibility by your personnel.

ACTION #3—VALIDATE BUSINESS, COMMUNITY, AND GOVERNMENT CONTACTS

The more you know about the support services upon which you depend, your organization's linkages to suppliers and customers, and your dependencies on critical infrastructures, the less apt your enterprise will be to assume too much. You should learn as much as you can about the critical infrastructures your enterprise depends on:

- electric power supplies
- gas and oil
- telecommunications
- banking and finance
- transportation
- water supply systems
- emergency services
- continuity of government

In addition to learning about and planning for critical infrastructure disruptions, your organization should get to know about the expectations and capabilities of your suppliers, business partners, and customers. (How would you deal with a situation in which one of your critical suppliers was not able to meet a scheduled delivery? What if a customer had an event and could not occupy their facilities? Would your organization be able to coordinate with the supplier or customer to the mutual satisfaction of all parties?)

You may wish to re-read chapter 2, as well as chapters 4 -6 as a refresher when undertaking this action.

ACTION #4—ASSESS BUSINESS CONTINUITY (STRATEGY, COMPETITIVE INTELLIGENCE, EVENT MANAGEMENT) INITIATIVES

Does your organization's current approach to business continuity employ the approach presented herein? Or are your plans segmented into a series of plans that are not integrated? Some key questions you may wish to ask yourself:

- Do we have a business continuity process that integrates strategy, competitive intelligence initiatives, and event management?
- Does our current event management system address all the threats, vulnerabilities, risks, and hazards that face our organization?
- Have we documented the potential consequence scenarios related to threat, vulnerability, risk, and hazard identification?
- How are our value chain relationships addressing the above questions?

If you have not integrated strategy, competitive intelligence, and event management into a business continuity system, or if you limited the focus to only a portion of your organization (such as information systems disaster recovery), you may want to rethink and rework your plans into an integrated business continuity system. An assessment of your program against the approach presented in this book may be the answer to the uncertainty you may be feeling. An integrated system will take into consideration strategy, competitive intelligence, and event management for your organization and its value chain.

ACTION #5—TRAIN AND EDUCATE YOUR WORKFORCE

A trained and educated workforce can do more to protect your enterprise than you can imagine. Training of personnel should be a critical component of any approach to business continuity. Training your personnel at all levels is a critical success factor that must be addressed if an adequate degree of protection is to be achieved. A "systems" approach to preparing effective training programs should consist of the following elements.

- Task analysis. When designing an integrated training program, first determine the skills, knowledge, and procedures required for satisfactory performance of each task

- Lesson development. Learning objectives are defined from the skills, knowledge, and procedures developed during task analysis. Instructional plans are then prepared to support the learning objectives

- Instruction. Lessons are systematically presented using appropriate instructional methods. Instruction may include lecture, self-paced, or group-paced mediated instruction, simulation, and team training

- Evaluation. Performance standards and evaluation criteria are developed from the learning objectives. Each trainee's performance is evaluated during the course and during field-performance testing

In addition to formal training, a program of proficiency demonstration is needed to validate the training and content of plans. This can be accomplished by establishing a program that supplements the training with simulations (drills and exercises).

Consider developing programs to educate your employees in basic life safety (first aid, CPR, evacuation, assembly, accountability); what to do if an event occurs; and what to do after the event. In addition, a community outreach program can provide your organization with many benefits. A program that enhances coordination with local emergency response and law enforcement agencies can put your organization in a positive light in the community and provide your employees more information on community resources.

ACTION #6—EQUIP YOUR WORKFORCE

You cannot stop at classroom training and expect your organization to respond effectively to an event. Corporate America needs to assess how prepared it is to deal with workplace events. The government must focus its attention on the protection of critical infrastructures and international issues.

Corporate America has to address protective measures that ensure its survival; it cannot depend blindly on the government to render assistance. And while being able to respond appropriately is and will be essential, responding without the proper equipment can lead to failure. You need to equip your workforce with the appropriate emergency response equipment, such as—

- first aid kits
- fire extinguishers
- event response kits
- evacuation, assembly, accountability procedures

You should also understand that when you purchase equipment and train your personnel on its use, you have to develop and implement a maintenance program to assure that the equipment is there and that it works when needed.

ACTION # 7—REVIEW LEASES AND CONTRACTS FOR RISK EXPOSURE

Every organization needs to completely assess its risk exposure. This includes both the standard risk exposure methodologies currently employed by your organization and all leases and contracts for potential risk exposure, specifically addressing the issue of terrorism and terrorism-related events. As described in previous chapters, the LMSCARVER™ analysis system provides an integrated approach to determining risk exposures.

ACTION # 8—ASSESS VALUE-CHAIN EXPOSURE TO SUPPLY DISRUPTIONS

Critical to all organizations is their value chain—all the internal/external "touchpoints" to suppliers, customers, outsourcing, strategic partners, and other entities that assure your organization's continued success. As with all critical infrastructure assessments, your organization needs to assess the potential effects of a disruption of its value chain to supply disruptions. In conducting the assessment, a variety of scenarios need to be developed, assessing the short-term, intermediate-term, and long-term effects of a disruption. The use of the LMSCARVER™ analysis system can facilitate the assessment process.

ACTION #9—REVIEW INSURANCE POLICIES AND CONDUCT COST/BENEFIT ANALYSIS

As a result of what occurred on Sept. 11, 2001 and subsequent events, a review of insurance policies with respect to coverage, exclusions, and exceptions needs to be accomplished. Insurance companies have been and will be impacted by the events of Sept. 11th and events yet to occur.

Many organizations will find that a cost/benefit analysis will offer an effective aid to decision-making, strategy planning, and the development of risk-reduction solutions. Again, by applying the LMSCARVER™ analysis tool to the evaluation, cost/benefit analysis can be finely tuned to reflect a clearer picture of true costs and benefits. Changes in insurance coverage for many organizations in what are deemed to be high risk/high exposure areas will potentially cause a financial burden for many organizations. This could lead to adverse effects on the organization's ability to maintain its business orientation, retain and/or increase staff, and continue to operate from current domicile locations.

ACTION #10—COMMUNICATE COMMITMENT

Without the support of the entire organization and your value chain, all the preparation and planning, the equipment and training, the liaison and information sharing will go for naught. From the highest level to the lowest, everyone in your organization must be kept well informed. Information is a corporate asset, and it's expensive. It must be shared and managed effectively.

Information management is also critical during an event. The need for active systems to provide information on materials, personnel, capabilities, and processes is essential. It is extremely important to have a system and adequate backup systems in place to identify, catalog, prioritize, and track issues and commitments relating to event management and response activities.

The need to communicate commitment throughout the organization on an ongoing basis is also very important. If your personnel feel that you are only giving lip service to preparedness, they are soon going to develop a lax attitude toward preparedness. Communicating commitment is an ongoing dynamic process that is cyclical and must be supported and actively worked on by all levels of the organization. Active participation can ensure operational resilience. The process doesn't end just because you finished your plan, have involved management, and have trained the staff.

Concluding Thoughts

We have discussed how to protect your organization.

When looking at these recommendations, you need to take into account the status of your organization's strategy, competitive intelligence initiatives, and event management capabilities. Included were examples of how to assess protection initiatives. As with previous chapters, this is intended to redefine business continuity thinking. After reading this chapter, you should be able to apply the concepts discussed and develop a strategy for protecting your organization and its value chain accessibility.

Trust and confidence in the abilities of all levels within your organization must be established. "How well do we integrate business continuity into our organization and our value chain?" is a question that can only be answered satisfactorily if you have established a level of trust and confidence; can communicate "risk," and are willing to allow your people to practice upward management—to delegate up. They must have the ability to recognize needs and have a process in place that allows them to delegate up without fear of repercussions.

You can ensure that all levels within the organization are involved in the business continuity process in several ways.

- Establish a formal business continuity program and assign the program to a senior manager directly responsible to top management and the board of directors

- Establish performance measurements throughout your organization that incorporate evaluations of continuity thinking. This goes both ways. Upper management has to take responsibility for developing measurable and attainable goals for the organization to achieve

- Set aside a specific time for reports on business continuity (strategy, competitive intelligence initiatives, and event management) issues. This can be accomplished by preparing an agenda for senior staff and board of directors' meetings including a discussion of business continuity as a mandatory item. You have to give it more than lip service, though, and you must make the discussion substantive, providing more than the dull and tiring statistics. Include all levels of personnel in the presentation process. This can very effectively get the message out to all personnel that your organization is serious about business continuity

- Make the strategic planning process, competitive intelligence, and event management activities an integrated part of the way you do business, instead of silos that turn into adjuncts to the business

- Communicate information on the importance of business continuity throughout all levels of your organization and the value chain. This can be accomplished through formal adoption of policies at the highest levels of the organization. The board of directors should endorse your business continuity initiatives

References

Davis, Stanley M., Christopher Meyer. *Blur: The Speed of Change in the Connected Economy*

Globalcontinuity.com Newsletter, 80 Percent of Companies Lack Information Availability Plans, June 2002 (www.globalcontinuity.com)

Lake, Anthony, *6 Nightmares*, 2000

Sikich, Geary W., Logical Management Systems, Corp. (www.logicalmanagement.com), LMSCARVER™ Touchpoint Analysis Diagnostic Program, 2000

———"September 11 Aftermath: Ten Things Your Organization Can Do Now," *John Liner Review,* Winter 2002, vol. 15, no. 4

———"Aftermath September 11th, Can Your Organization Afford to Wait?" New York State Bar Association, Federal and Commercial Litigation, Spring Conference, May 2002

———"September 11th, Can Your Organization Afford to Wait?" GlobalContinuity.com, May 2002

———"Ten Things Your Organization Can do Now!" The International Emergency Management Society, 9th Annual Conference Proceedings, May 2002

Chapter Nine

KNOWLEDGE MANAGEMENT: EFFECTIVE COMMUNICATIONS IN THE "AGE OF THE INSTANT"

Chapter Summary

In this chapter, we will discuss knowledge management and effective communications.

While we live in an age of near-instantaneous information, just "accessing information" is not the same thing as "gaining knowledge." Having knowledge does not mean that you can effectively communicate the information you have. How can you effectively identify, manage, and communicate information to your key publics before they are inundated with potential misinformation from other sources? This chapter will assist you in identifying information, managing knowledge, developing your message, and effectively communicating messages to your key stakeholders. Discussed will be:

- knowledge and knowledge management
- need to know—nice to know

DEFINITION OF TERMS USED IN THIS CHAPTER

Crisis communications
Communication under duress

Stakeholders
Entities with a vested interest in your organization

Data mining
Analysis technique for very large databases

Knowledge
Familiarity, awareness, or understanding

Knowledge base
Organized structures of information

Knowledge management
Process of managing and presenting information

Need to know
Essential information for decision making

Nice to know
Information that does not necessarily direct decisions

- communicating knowledge without giving away the store

This chapter is intended to help you to identify knowledge sources, establish knowledge management systems, and identify those groups that you have to communicate with that are key to your organization's survival. The outcome you should achieve is a concept for the structure and application of knowledge and effective communications to your business continuity plan for various levels of your organization.

Crisis communications. Communication of information under duress or when the organization is experiencing disruption.

Stakeholders. Key audiences for your organization.

Data mining. Analysis technique for very large databases that can reveal trends and patterns and can be used to improve vital business processes.

Knowledge. The *American Heritage Dictionary* defines knowledge as the familiarity, awareness, or understanding gained through experience or study.

Knowledge base. Organized structures of information that facilitate intelligence storage in order to be retrieved in support of a knowledge management process.

Knowledge management. Systematic process of finding, selecting, organizing, distilling, and presenting information in a way that improves comprehension in a specific area of interest.

Need to know. Essential information for decision making.

Nice to know. Information that does not necessarily direct decisions. However this information may be an influencing factor for decision makers.

Introduction

As I begin this chapter, I was reminded of *MAD* magazine's long running "Spy vs. Spy" series created by the late, legendary cartoonist Antonio Prohias. For more than four decades, the black Spy and white Spy built their bizarre, elaborate contraptions and entertained us with their antics. As business moves forward in the information age, the never-ending scheming of the Spies seems as relevant as ever.

We have seen that, today, more than ever before, we are inundated with sources of information. The challenge is to turn information sources into intelligence that can be used by an organization to establish and maintain a competitive edge. Effective knowledge management coupled with excellent communication will play an ever more integral role in every successful business.

Obtaining information about your company isn't too difficult. But, because there is so much information competing for attention, it is often difficult to "punch through the noise" and reach an audience. Therefore, it is your challenge as an organization to keep your stakeholders and value chain in the information loop.

Your organization's primary knowledge management objective should be to get the right message to the right audience in a believable way. Before you can deliver a message, it is essential to complete the following steps:

- identify and analyze your target audiences
- set your knowledge management and communications objectives
- develop your messages

Knowledge and Knowledge Management

According to *Webster's Dictionary*, knowledge is "the fact or condition of knowing something with familiarity gained through experience or association." Knowledge can be recorded and stored in an individual's brain or found in an organization's policies, processes, services, products, systems, and documents. The University of Texas at Austin provides the following definition from a project on knowledge management:

...the ideas or understandings that an entity possesses that are used to take effective action to achieve the entity's goal(s).

Based on this definition, knowledge is specific to the entity that created it. Knowledge, however created, is not useful in and of itself; knowledge must be transformed into action before it can be useful. Just "knowing something" does not mean that you will gain, lose, or create advantage for your organization. In order for knowledge to be effective, it must be put to use in a way so that the organization benefits from its application.

In today's fast-paced world, an organization's knowledge base—its collective intelligence—is quickly becoming its only sustainable competitive advantage. As such, this intelligence base must be protected, cultivated, and shared within the value chain of the organization. Strategy, competitive intelligence, and event management have traditionally been viewed as separate elements, if not completely distinct in some organizations. Small groups of strategically positioned individuals in organizations have combined strategy and competitive intelligence initiatives to achieve success, only to be thwarted by an event that disrupted the value chain and changed the course of strategy and competitive intelligence. As a result, competitors were able to offer a better knowledge proposition as part of their services. You may ask "How?" Simply put, the competition gains a competitive advantage because during the event, the organization bled so much information (knowledge) that the competition was able to capitalize on the situation without going to significant effort to secure a competitive edge.

By combining strategy, competitive intelligence, and event management into a business continuity framework, you can leverage organizational knowledge by making it more responsive and less apt to unknowingly give away information that can become a competitive advantage for another entity. The full utilization of your organization's knowledge base to fulfill its strategy and competitive intelligence initiatives, and manage potentially disruptive events can enable it to compete more effectively in the future.

The University of Texas project also cited:

Specific knowledge management activities help focus the organization on acquiring, storing and utilizing knowledge for such things

*as problem solving, dynamic learning, strategic planning and deci-
sion making. It also protects intellectual assets from decay, adds to
firm intelligence and provides increased flexibility.*

This is a key point to consider as you develop your business continuity
thought process from an organizational standpoint. Everyone in the organization and its value chain must have the same appreciation and understanding
of the value of knowledge (intelligence). Only after this understanding is
achieved can seamless vertical and horizontal communications be created.
This seamless communication process based on common terminology and
knowledge management becomes a way of achieving business success and
assures business continuity.

The definition of a certified knowledge engineer comes to mind again. It is
based on modeling how one knows what they know, how they know that they
know what they know, and how they know that someone else can know what
they know. Simply put, "I know what I know, because I know what I know and
know that someone else knows that I know what I know." This may sound like
Popeye the sailor talking, but it has some real application to redefining business
continuity and how we manage knowledge in our organization and its value
chain. Many organizations do not "know what they know." Such situations can
often lead to loss of strategic direction, competitive intelligence leaks, duplica-
tion of efforts, and chaos and confusion in dealing with events.

Two important questions are asked in the University of Texas project:

- "What are our knowledge assets?"
- "How should we manage those assets to ensure a maximum return on them?"

While the University of Texas team claims there are no right or wrong
answers to these questions, they indicate that "Solutions will depend upon
several factors such as the type of organization, its culture and its needs."

Effective business continuity—the integration of strategy, competitive intelligence, and event management—will focus on solutions encompassing the
organization and its value chain. The integration of strategy, competitive intelligence, and event management into a comprehensive business continuity system can radically improve decision-making, resource allocation, value chain
relationships, information access, and security. In this way, core competencies can be leveraged to achieve maximum effectiveness.

Need to Know—Nice to Know

Any organization can collect information and turn it into knowledge. The question that must be asked is: "How do we effectively transform that information and knowledge into usable intelligence?" A follow-on question should be, "Once we have usable intelligence, how do we make it available to the organization in such a way so not to create competitive intelligence vulnerabilities?" Lastly: "How do we use this intelligence to effectively make decisions that enhance business continuity?"

Hewlett Packard, for example, has created a system known as "Knowledge Links" that is used to identify, categorize, and store important company knowledge. This knowledge is accessible by any employee within the company. When we look at organizational restructuring in today's business environment, we clearly see a need to assure the security of such organizational knowledge.

You may recall that one of the early assumptions cited in this book related to the complexity of business systems and their operation in networks that are also complex. I further cited that unless all systems' touchpoints within a given network could be identified and analyzed, the network would not function well. James Gleick's book, *Chaos* (1987) discusses the science of "non-linear systems," throwing open the doors of unpredictability regarding turbulent natural events that cannot be predicted as a result of chaos. For example, he says that no matter how much data are collected about weather, the best we can do is get an estimate of what weather will be like in a day or two. What first appears simple is rendered incomprehensible by the presence of chaos. The tiniest fluctuation in any one of thousands of variables (influences) can dramatically alter the course in ways that cannot be anticipated.

"Chaos theory" is not confined to natural phenomena like the weather. Gleick cites many examples of chaotic systems, such as economics, human relationships, political movements, and cultural trends, to name a few. The key point to remember is that chaotic systems are extremely sensitive to small changes. Based on my definition of business continuity, the challenge for decision-makers will be to harness knowledge into intelligence and make use of intelligence in such a way so as to minimize disruption to the system (organization) and the network (value chain) that it operates in.

Again, we are inundated with information; today, just about anybody can find out anything they want to know, just by accessing an Internet search engine and typing in a few "key words." It seems there's so much to know. Organizations need to develop mechanisms that screen the wealth of available information and turn it into intelligence that can be used in decision-making.

Any organization that can figure out how to manage network complexity and maximize decision-making—at the point and time needed—can position itself to compete more effectively and succeed much faster. Many executives and their employees have vital knowledge resting within them and do little to make the knowledge more generally available. Many organizations are unaware of the knowledge base existing in the organization and its value chain. Evidence has shown that knowledge is often lost from an organization through employee attrition or related cost-saving measures. The organization (including its value chain) that can harness its intellectual capital and apply that asset to its business challenges and opportunities will achieve business continuity.

Determining what is "need to know" versus "nice to know" can be accomplished by integrating strategy, competitive intelligence initiatives, and event management. Having an effective system in place that collects, collates, analyzes, filters, and distributes information to users is not as daunting a task as it may seem. The military forces of countries around the world from the earliest of times have often accomplished this task. By integrating strategy, competitive intelligence, and event management, we can react to and manage chaotic systems better.

If, as Brian Muldoon writes in his book, *The Heart of Conflict,* "Chaotic systems are extremely sensitive to small changes," then organizations must be better prepared to identify events in their preliminary stages and track them in order to avoid having to respond to those chaotic situations. This requires that organizations begin to think of business continuity not as an adjunct to the business, but as a way of doing business. Being able to identify the small changes and the potential impacts they may have on your organization and its value chain can be one of the most valuable assets your organization can possess. It will help you differentiate the need to know, from the nice to know and it will facilitate the organization's ability to be resilient and responsive—two of the criteria from my redefinition of business continuity.

Table 9-1 is an example of a simplified need to know—nice to know event-tracking methodology.

Distribution	Source	Need to Know	Nice to Know	Disposition
Who gets the information Distribution may be based on source, sensitivity, and application of the information	Unique identifier code for the source and synopsis (key words, etc.) of the information	Identifies who made determination and on what basis Also restricts the pool of who sees the information	Identifies who made determination and on what basis Enables distribution based on sensitivity of the information	What is to be done with the information (reclassify, take action, redistribute, etc.)

Table 9-1 Need to Know vs. Nice to Know

The benefit of establishing a need to know—nice to know system is that your organization can study the flow of information and establish communication channels to facilitate enhancement of information distribution and analysis. It can also enhance the disposition of information to enable the information to be turned into intelligence that aids the decision-making process—not inhibits it.

COMMUNICATING KNOWLEDGE WITHOUT GIVING AWAY THE STORE

In differentiating between "need to know" and "nice to know," we see that information is essential and yet can be overwhelming. Our quandary is how do we communicate knowledge (intelligence) in such a way that we do not give away the "store" in the process.

By "giving away the store" I am referring to the unintentional disclosure of the source of the intelligence. Often times, the source is actually more important in the long run than the immediate intelligence. In this section, I am going to focus on techniques that will enable your organization to communicate intelligence more effectively. Some of these techniques are the same as those practiced by spokespersons. There is a reason for that. It particularly deals with the audience (stakeholders) with whom you are communicating.

I use this statement to introduce the subject of communicating during an event ("crisis"):

> *The length of time you will have to react to an event is directly related to its perceived impact on your organization by your key publics.*

In an earlier chapter, I introduced the aspect of speed, connectivity, and intangibles. We live in a world that is increasingly becoming obsessed with speed. It may seem that "everyone wants it now" is an appropriate phrase. The truth is that we have been fortunate that infrastructures supporting the speed and connectivity that we crave via the Internet, telecommunications, and media have been able to support the growing dependence we place on information processing. If ever there is a significant disruption of the interlaced infrastructure systems, we may find ourselves incapable of managing the communication process effectively. By "disruption" I am not referring to a major attack on the systems.

Recall that I wrote earlier that we (the U.S.) have reduced our energy refining capacity by more than 53%; we have a utility grid system that is interdependent. Our telecommunications infrastructure is undergoing significant change (*i.e.*, WorldCom), and the transportation system is still attempting to recover and respond to the "new threat" environment.

Effective communication is based on the sender's ability to formulate messages that are understood by the recipient. Consider this: Ideas get distorted in the transmission process.

Typically we remember:

- 10% of what we hear
- 35% of what we see
- 65% of what we see *and* hear

Typically we spend:

- 30% speaking
- 9% writing
- 16% reading
- 45% listening

One has to wonder, if we spend 45% of our time listening, why is it that we only remember 10% of what we hear?

A number of years ago, I heard Anthony Robbins speak at a conference. He understands the need to communicate effectively. In his presentation, he pointed out that words by themselves are approximately 7% effective. So as you read this book, I realize that my words alone are only going to have minimal effect. Robbins also pointed out that voice tonality (sound) can bring the effectiveness of communications up to approximately 38%. So, if I can get you to read the words and listen to this book on tape or some other recorded media, my effectiveness is going to be far greater, simply based on tonality. He further stated that physiology (gestures, movement, etc.) can bring us to approximately 55% effectiveness in communicating. While this impressed me, I find that it still leaves us with a quandary: How do we combine words, tonality, and physiology to create the most effective communication vehicle? How do we do so in such a manner that we do not disclose information (intelligence), giving our competition an advantage?

In his book, *World Without Secrets: Business, Crime, and Privacy in the Age of Ubiquitous Computing*, Richard Hunter describes the *mentat*, the "human" thinking machine first invented by novelist Frank Herbert for his science fiction classic *Dune*. Mentats assimilate vast quantities of information and provide us with concise advice; they guide us rapidly to effective decisions, hiding the details. Hunter writes, "No one wants more information. Information is so common that it's oppressive and annoying." This often leads to a phenomenon known as "information overload."

A colleague of mine uses a rule that can be applied very effectively to the event management and competitive intelligence aspects of business continuity as I am defining it. The rule is simple: 20 - 2 - 20. You will spend approximately 20 seconds on something that gets your attention. You will take 2 minutes to decide on whether you want to continue assessing the item (investing your time), and you will spend approximately 20 minutes assessing the information for applicability. For many of us, the processing time is far less and, as such, may be far less effective.

An American Management Association survey provided a statistic that more than 70% of an executive's time is spent "putting out fires" (crises; dealing with unexpected events). If we agree that crisis (an event that gets our attention and must be dealt with) is a part of doing business, and that every crisis is a violation of strategy (mission, vision, values) and a potential competitive intelligence (our organization gets unwanted exposure) windfall to our competition, then we have to address the need to effectively integrate strategy, competitive intelligence, and event management into a business continuity philosophy that is effectively communicated throughout the organization and its value chain.

As an event unfolds, we are often faced with information overload, which leads to decision-making paralysis: It is easier not to decide than to have to decide. Deciding what matters, why, and how it matters before making a decision can be a daunting task. Strategy and competitive intelligence initiatives are pushed to the wayside as you wrestle with the event at hand. (As an example: As I write this, the stock market is seemingly rocked by one revelation of potential corporate impropriety after another.)

Your audience sees and hears exactly what they want to see and hear, not necessarily what you show them or say to them. They do not know what goes into your decision-making. Your competition is looking at your message and picking it apart to determine what your audience is "not" seeing or hearing.

Effectively communicating to your audience while keeping competitive intelligence information excluded from your competition's view is especially important when your competition's real agenda is hidden from the user, when the competition's purpose is not to "inform" but to "mislead." Your competition will do everything they can to effectively use your event to their advantage. If a perception can be created that your organization is in turmoil, they can often times gain market share. We live in a world of sound bites; even if your competition cannot keep market share gains for the long term, the leverage that can be had in the short duration can effectively go to their bottom line. Very few events become institutionalized. Generally, they are not as spectacular and therefore not destined to become a lasting memory.

Your organization needs to communicate with many target audiences, typically including:

- shareholders, investors, mutual funds, other shareholder groups
- board of directors
- corporate officers/management, senior, executive, mid-level, junior-level management
- retirees
- families of employees
- suppliers

- existing and potential customers
- contractors and subcontractors
- regulatory community (federal, state, local)
- community at large
- banking/financial community
- healthcare providers
- insurers
- media
- consumers
- facilities/landlord
- utilities (gas, electric, water)
- telecommunication systems providers
- mail providers
- specialty service providers
- competitors
- analysts
- government officials

On certain occasions, however, you may need to concentrate on a few principal targets, depending on the circumstances, the time available, or the type of information being communicated. A television interview, for example, will reach a different audience than the business column of a newspaper.

The first step in communicating knowledge without giving up the store is to identify your audience. The next step is to identify who or what are the conduits for delivering your message to your audience. Once these two steps have been accomplished, you need to set communication objectives. Your communication objectives should be measurable and observable action(s) that you want your audience to take. Without a clear idea of communication objectives, you cannot effectively communicate. As a colleague of mine once said, "Are we trying to put bullet holes in the bulls-eye or bulls-eyes over the bullet holes?" Or as I have said, "If you do not have a target, you are sure to hit it."

After you have determined your target audience, ask yourself what actions you'd like them to take as a result of hearing you or reading your communication. Only when you have your communication objectives firmly in mind can you develop the messages that will cause your audience to act in a way that will accomplish your communications objectives.

Once you have established communication objectives, you may think you can begin to develop the messages you want to communicate to your target audiences. However, you may find it useful to put your objectives into better focus by listing the facts, perceptions, beliefs, and even the rumors that could be brought up when communicating your message.

I have found that it is effective to use a two-column format. I list all the positives and negatives I can think of. If there are positives I can use to respond to some of the negatives, I am already on my way to developing the message needed to reach my communication objective.

The next step is to develop the message. First you must recognize that there is a proliferation of media inundating audiences with information. Because of information overload, people tend to selectively listen—to tune out much of what they hear. On average, people retain less than 10% of the information they receive; therefore, to reach your communication objectives, it is imperative to develop concise messages that you want your audience to hear and remember. Your message should be not just concise, but attention getting and memorable. It should have a primary communications objective (PCO) that your audience can readily identify. You need to support your message with:

- facts—simple statements that describe the way things are

- statistics—when used sparingly, statistics are most effective when put into easy-to-understand terms

- authorities or experts—quoting an expert adds credibility to any message, especially if the expert is a disinterested third party

- analogy or comparison—using an analogy or comparison between two things makes the message more memorable

- personal experience—employing personal experience to illustrate your point enables your audience to relate to and comprehend your message

Ready to deliver your message? One of the keys to having your message retained by your target audience is repetition. It is to your advantage to get your primary communication objective reinforced as many times as possible in the message.

There are several fine books written on the topic of public speaking, and there are many organizations that specialize in preparing spokespersons to address the media. I am not going to attempt to cover presentation techniques in detail here, because you can readily access the books, courses, and consulting services that are offered. I will offer some simple guidelines for effective communications:

- Talk from the viewpoint of your audience's interest. This means that you have to know your audience

- Do not use jargon—it can be confusing, and what makes sense to you may mean something entirely different to someone else. For example, DOS means disk operating system to many, however to others DOS means denial of service. Jargon can create problems!

- Identify conduits to your audience and do not mistake them for your audience

- Communicate in terms that enhance credibility

- If you do not want information quoted, do not make it available

If intelligence is the refined product of information gathering, communicating intelligence is what allows your organization to survive, grow, and remain resilient. Effective communication of your organization's message to and throughout its value chain will enhance business continuity.

Concluding Thoughts

We discussed "how to manage knowledge and communicate intelligence without giving away the store." The process of information gathering and its subsequent transformation into usable intelligence are important to your organization's business continuity. Please note that emphasis is on the word "usable" in the previous sentence. Intelligence without a purpose or use is merely noise. In today's business environment, organizations cannot afford to have noise clutter the decision-making process. They cannot afford to have noise clutter the communication channels within the organization, through to its value chain, and to its various stakeholders.

You may wish to ask yourself, "How do we communicate our strategy, competitive intelligence initiatives, and event management capabilities?" The answers you get may surprise you.

Included in this chapter are examples of knowledge and knowledge management, how to differentiate "need to know" from "nice to know," and how to communicate without giving away intelligence. This chapter is intended to introduce potentially innovative applications of concepts that are not necessarily new, but have not been effectively applied to business continuity as I am defining it. By reading this chapter, you should be able to apply these concepts to more effectively communicate within your organization and its value chain. Integrating business continuity into your organization and its value chain is a process that must become a way of doing business, not an afterthought.

References

American Management Society, Survey Results, 1987

Gleick, James. *Chaos*, 1987

Herbert, Frank. *Dune*

Hewlett Packard. "Knowledge Links"

Hunter, Richard. *Privacy in the Age of Ubiquitous Computing*
———World Without Secrets

Muldoon, Brian. *The Heart of Conflict*, 1996

Prohais, Antonio, Spy vs. Spy, *Mad* magazine (four decades worth of laughter)

Robbins, Anthony, "Unleash The Power Within," seminar
———University of Texas at Austin, Knowledge Management Project Report of Results

Sikich, Geary W. *It Can't Happen Here: All Hazards Crisis Management Planning*, PennWell Publishing, 1993
———*The Emergency Management Planning Handbook*, McGraw-Hill Books, 1995
———Logical Management Systems, Corp. AUDITRAK^{tm} Diagnostic Assessment Program (www.logicalmanagement.com)
———Managing Crisis at the Speed of Light, Disaster Recovery Journal Conference, 1999

Webster's New World Dictionary, definition of knowledge

Chapter Ten

THE NEXT WAVE: GLOBAL VULNERABILITIES, LOCAL IMPACTS

Chapter Summary

In this chapter, we will discuss scenarios for future crisis situations—scenarios that are unfolding even as this manuscript is being written. Included are examples of scenarios that you can use to assess the adequacy and effectiveness of your organization's approach to business continuity. These scenarios include, but are not limited to:

- government relations
- corporate relations
- corporate image
- banking and finance
- international conflict
- loss of critical infrastructures
- operational events

- terrorism
- workplace violence

This chapter is intended to help you to develop scenarios that your organization can use to answer the "what if" questions that business continuity management planners should be constantly asking. The outcome you should achieve is a concept for integrating strategy, competitive intelligence initiatives, and event management into a comprehensive business continuity system. The integration of business continuity should extend vertically and horizontally within the various levels of your organization and through to your value chain.

Scenario. A scenario is a creative activity that is the underlying driver for simulations designed to validate the strategy, competitive intelligence, and event management components of business continuity.

A scenario is also a creative tool used for the assessment and analysis steps that underlie the basic assumptions of the business continuity process.

Worst case. Worst-case scenarios are theoretical sequences of events intentionally devised to be as bad as possible. Worst-case scenarios are creative exercises, not predictions of likely events.

Most likely case. Most-likely-case scenarios are also theoretical sequences of events; however, they are intentionally devised to be reflective of known outcomes. Most-likely-case scenarios are also creative exercises, based on what has happened in the past.

Best case. Best-case scenarios are also theoretical sequences of events; however, they are intentionally devised to be reflective of optimum/desired outcomes. Best-case scenarios are creative exercises, based on the most desired sequence of steps allowing for achieving maximum/optimum outcomes.

Critical thinking. Critical thinking is the ability to see problems from multiple perspectives, expose critical underlying assumptions, challenge and reverse one's assumptions, and reformulate basic arguments.

Data fusion. The bringing together of diverse and often times seemingly unrelated pieces of information to form a "comprehensive" package for analysis. Data fusion requires seamless communication, intense scrutiny of data for applicability, and the ability to visualize the application of the data as information to aid decision-making throughout the organization.

Introduction

In his book, *The Six Nightmares*, Anthony Lake presents on overview of threats facing America and how they can be addressed. I would suggest that we begin to "think globally and act locally," rather than just focusing on the United States of America, because the threats we face today are worldwide in their scope. The actors (you may read this as "the bad guys") know and respect no boundaries. As such, business and government need to establish a close working relationship to ensure each other's continuity and global stability.

Business cannot operate effectively without government support. Government cannot operate without business support in the form of taxes and regulatory compliance. The public is dependent on business and government to maintain a standard of living. Business and government are dependent on the public to supply the workforce and administrators to keep things going.

Mr. Lake cites six threats (or nightmares as he refers to them) in his book:

- new tools for new terrorists
- eTerror, eCrime
- ambiguous warfare
- peacekeeping as a permanent band-aid
- the perils of weakness
- the sixth nightmare—Washington, D.C.

I highly recommend Mr. Lake's book, as it is informative and enlightening. I will not attempt to restate the six nightmares from his book in this chapter.

I will, however, discuss my perspectives on some of the same nightmares and the threats they present.

Similarly, *Fear Less,* by Gavin De Becker, deals with, as is stated on the cover, "Real truth about risk, safety, and security in a time of terrorism." In the book are chapters addressing:

- the illusion of powerlessness
- being anti-terrorist—the messengers of intuition
- being anti-terrorist—the architecture of conspiracy
- apocalypse not now
- safer than driving to the airport— still
- no news at 11
- the newsspeak of fear

I highly recommend Mr. De Becker's books as entertaining and enlightening. Again, I will not attempt to restate the material from Mr. De Becker's books in this chapter; however, I will discuss my perspectives on some of the material presented.

I want to alert you to two other books that are extremely good reading: *Catch Me If You Can* and *The Art of the Steal,* both by Frank Abagnale. Frank is a gifted storyteller and his books read quickly. He is also an expert in fraud. I actually read his second book *The Art of the Steal* first and was so fascinated I went back and got his first book. Frank's message deals with what he terms "one of the biggest crime growth areas"—identity theft and fraud.

Lastly, I think that reading Arianna Huffington's book, *How to Overthrow the Government* will round out the reading selections. This is a book that, as you read it, you sometimes wonder, "Did she make this stuff up?", then you realize that it is all too true and frightening.

There you have it—my recommendations for a little light reading. You may be wondering why I started this chapter with such a diverse list of recommendations for reading. As a former intelligence officer, I learned that you have to have multiple sources of information to develop a complete picture of intentions, trends, threats, etc. I also learned that seemingly unrelated pieces of information could be put together to build a "complete" analysis.

This is *data fusion*—the bringing together of diverse and often seemingly unrelated pieces of information to form a comprehensive package for analysis. The reading recommendations and other works cited are examples of diverse and often seemingly unrelated information sources that have the threads or bits and pieces of information that can be assembled, analyzed and applied to decision-making. Further stated in the definition of data fusion is that seamless communication, intense scrutiny of data for applicability, and the ability to visualize the application of the data as information to aid decision-making throughout the organization are required. Without communication, data are often kept in the departmental "silo." Without communication, you are not likely to know if others can use the information.

Tables 10-1 through 10-5 are scenarios used to introduce a simulation on workplace violence. I take a group of participants and subdivide them into five teams. Each team gets one of five pieces of information. Then we discuss the information provided. Each participant group presents their conclusions after they analyze the information. As I present the scenario, I never restrict the groups from discussing the information they are provided with members of the other groups. Interestingly enough, the participants always stay within their group and prepare discussion and analysis points based on the single piece of information they are provided. The result is that when each group begins to present its findings and assessment, five very different conclusions result.

Workplace Violence Scenario	What You Know	(1)
Lester is a 44-year-old white male who does skilled labor at a service company. He has been employed there for 28 years with an exceptionally good attendance record. He lives alone in his own home in a suburb and has never been married. He is very intelligent and follows a predictable pattern much of the day. He generally stays to himself at work, although there is one man whom he spends time with at work. He is sometimes the brunt of practical jokes played by his co-workers. He can be difficult in that he withholds cooperation on projects, making it impossible for others to complete their work. He frequently complains to the union steward, sometimes in the form of formal grievances, which he generally wins. Currently, he is looking to make a lateral move within the company and is competing with another person for the job. He has made intimidating comments to the other person (female) who is frightened of him. The comments include: "I'm better qualified for the job than you are!" "Who did you screw to try to get the job?" The receptionist reports to you that she generally takes an early lunch. One day, the large lunchroom was empty and Lester comes in and takes a seat directly across from her. He is reading a book that he holds up so she can clearly see the title, which is *Men Who Love To Kill Women*. She said, "It gave me chill bumps." He said nothing.		
Please answer, in writing, the following questions:		
Do you think Lester is dangerous? Why?		
What, if anything, do you think should be done to further investigate or to handle this situation? What is the next step(s)?		

Table 10–1 Workplace Violence Scenario Information Sequence #1

Workplace Violence Scenario	What You Know	(2)
Lester is a 44-year-old white male who does skilled labor at a service company. He has been employed there for 28 years with an exceptionally good attendance record. He lives alone in his own home in a suburb and has never been married. He is very intelligent and follows a predictable pattern much of the day. He generally stays to himself at work, although there is one man whom he spends time with at work. He is sometimes the brunt of practical jokes played by his co-workers. He can be difficult in that he withholds cooperation on projects, making it impossible for others to complete their work. He frequently complains to the union steward, sometimes in the form of formal grievances, which he generally wins. Currently, he is looking to make a lateral move within the company and is competing with another person for the job. They have had a verbal confrontation where Lester made intimidating comments to the other person (female). The comments include: "I'm better qualified for the job than you are," "Who did you screw to try to get the job?" The supervisor, who has alternately befriended and come down hard on Lester, tells you when you inquire about any family information he may have on Lester, that he has a twin sister. The supervisor found out through the sister that Lester was given to a neighbor to raise shortly after their birth. He returned to his mother's home (the father by then was deceased, cause unknown) at age seven when the neighbor moved. He was frequently disciplined by being locked in a dark basement. Mother clearly favored his sister, and prior to his mother's death, mother and son had a love-hate relationship. Lester seldom sees or talks to his sister.		

Please answer, in writing, the following questions:	
Do you think Lester is dangerous? Why?	
What, if anything, do you think should be done to further investigate or to handle this situation? What is the next step(s)?	

Table 10–2 Workplace Violence Scenario Information Sequence #2

Workplace Violence Scenario	What You Know	(3)
Lester is a 44-year-old white male who does skilled labor at a service company. He has been employed there for 28 years with an exceptionally good attendance record. He lives alone in his own home in a suburb and has never been married. He is very intelligent and follows a predictable pattern much of the day. He generally stays to himself at work, although there is one man whom he spends time with at work. He is sometimes the brunt of practical jokes played by his co-workers. He can be difficult in that he withholds cooperation on projects, making it impossible for others to complete their work. He frequently complains to the union steward, sometimes in the form of formal grievances, which he generally wins. Currently, he is looking to make a lateral move within the company and is competing with another person for the job. The other person competing for the job is a female, who has had a confrontation with Lester. The confrontation, you are told, included the following comments from Lester: "I'm better qualified for the job than you are." "Women should be at home, barefoot, and pregnant, not in the workplace taking jobs from people who need the work!"

One of Lester's co-workers reports to you that Lester has made other comments regarding how much more qualified he is for the job than the other applicants. The co-worker indicates that Lester feels he has a lock on the position and has already purchased some items on credit with the plan of paying them off with the additional salary he expects. The co-worker indicates that if Lester does not get the job, he might take it very hard. | | |
Please answer, in writing, the following questions:		
Do you think Lester is dangerous? Why?		
What, if anything, do you think should be done to further investigate or to handle this situation? What is the next step(s)?		

Table 10–3 Workplace Violence Scenario Information Sequence #3

Workplace Violence Scenario	What You Know	(4)
Lester is a 44-year-old white male who does skilled labor at a service company. He has been employed there for 28 years with an exceptionally good attendance record. He lives alone in his own home in a suburb and has never been married. He is very intelligent and follows a predictable pattern much of the day. He generally stays to himself at work, although there is one man whom he spends time with at work. He is sometimes the brunt of practical jokes played by his co-workers. He can be difficult in that he withholds cooperation on projects, making it impossible for others to complete their work. He frequently complains to the union steward, sometimes in the form of formal grievances, which he generally wins. Currently, he is looking to make a lateral move within the company and is competing with another person for the job. He has made intimidating comments to the other person (female), who is frightened of him. The comments include: "I'm better qualified for the job than you are," "Who did you screw to try to get the job?"		
A co-worker, who has befriended Lester, tells you when you inquire that he and Lester are avid gun collectors. The co-worker and Lester go target shooting about twice a month. The co-worker indicates that Lester is not a very good shot, however, Lester seems to take his advice and says he is practicing for a match coming up soon. The co-worker indicates that he knows of no match scheduled in the area. He adds that Lester always refers to his targets in female terms. Lester seldom sees or talks to other employees.		

Please answer, in writing, the following questions:	
Do you think Lester is dangerous? Why?	
What, if anything, do you think should be done to further investigate or to handle this situation? What is the next step(s)?	

Table 10–4 Workplace Violence Scenario Information Sequence #4

As you can see by reading each piece of information and analyzing it separately—instead of combining the five pieces of information to form a whole—a very different picture of Lester emerges. This is why data fusion can be so important to an organization. It also points out a challenge for today's organization: assembling information into a cohesive and useable form.

In today's diverse organization, with its extended value chain, this challenge is growing, as evidenced by the bits and pieces of information that various governmental agencies had prior to Sept. 11, 2001. This is not to point a finger

Workplace Violence Scenario	What You Know	(5)
Lester is a 44-year-old white male who does skilled labor at a service company. He has been employed there for 28 years with an exceptionally good attendance record. He lives alone in his own home in a suburb and has never been married. He is very intelligent and follows a predictable pattern much of the day. He generally stays to himself at work, although there is one man whom he spends time with at work. He is often the brunt of practical jokes played by his co-workers. He can be difficult in that he withholds cooperation on projects, making it impossible for others to complete their work. He frequently complains to the union steward, sometimes in the form of formal grievances, which he generally wins. Currently, he is looking to make a lateral move within the company and is competing with another person for the job. He has made intimidating comments to other workers indicating that he better get the job and that the other person (female) is totally unqualified for the job. A co-worker tells you when you inquire that Lester has recently erected a makeshift partition around his work area, claiming that he is getting severe headaches from the radio waves emanating from his supervisor's monitoring equipment. The co-worker also indicates that Lester found out through one of the other workers that he might not get the promotion he is expecting. The co-worker also indicates that Lester has been reading a book dealing with alien abduction cases. The co-worker laughs and tells you that Lester can be a real handful at times.		
Please answer, in writing, the following questions:		
Do you think Lester is dangerous? Why?		
What, if anything, do you think should be done to further investigate or to handle this situation? What is the next step(s)?		

Table 10–5 Workplace Violence Scenario Information Sequence #5

at the government, as I firmly believe the events of that day could not have been stopped. Rather, it is to point out that without data fusion, much information an organization has available to it will go to naught unless it is communicated throughout the organization and continuously scrutinized by decision-makers. My point in providing the reading recommendations and the workplace violence exercise as an example is that diverse sources of information and views offer an interesting cross-section of information that can be used to develop inputs to your business continuity efforts if they are properly analyzed, shared, communicated, and used in the decision-making process.

Scenarios—What Are They?

There are two basic types of scenarios that I employ: simulation and "what if" scenarios. These two types of scenarios consist of three components—worst case, most-likely case, and best case—as depicted in Figures 10-1 through 10-3.

Create a record of your nightmares:

Worst-case scenarios are theoretical sequences of events intentionally devised to be as bad as possible

Worst-case scenarios are creative exercises, not predictions of likely events

Copyright 2002, all rights reserved, Logical Management Systems, Corp.

Fig. 10–1 Worst-Case Scenario

Explore the realities of your world:

Most-likely-case scenarios are also theoretical sequences of events, however they are intentionally devised to be reflective of known outcomes

Most-likely-case scenarios are also creative exercises, based on what has happened in the past

Copyright 2002, all rights reserved, Logical Management Systems, Corp.

Fig. 10–2 Most-Likely-Case Scenario

Determine the Optimum Desired Outcome:

Best-case scenarios are also theoretical sequences of events, however they are intentionally devised to be reflective of optimum/desired outcomes. Best-case scenarios are creative exercises, based on the most desired sequence of steps that allow for achieving maximum/optimum outcomes.

Fig. 10–3 Best-Case Scenario

The first type is the simulation scenario, created as the basis for a simulation designed to evaluate business continuity. This type of scenario is generally associated with the event management component of business continuity. The second type of scenario, "what if" scenario, is designed to provide a sequence for the analysis process and is more often used in the strategy and competitive intelligence components of business continuity. I also use the "what if" type of scenario when I develop the analysis and assessment portion of the event management component.

SIMULATION SCENARIOS

One way to develop better decision-making processes throughout the organization and its value chain is to create scenarios simulating events requiring individuals to react, make decisions, implement actions, and effectively communicate those decisions to a variety of stakeholders. This type of scenario-based simulation is very effective in validating the components of business continuity.

I have defined a scenario as a creative exercise that is the underlying driver for a potential sequence of events designed to validate the strategy, competitive intelligence, and event management components of business continuity. In the subsequent sections of this chapter, I will discuss the process for scenario development and the conduct of simulations. The goal is to integrate vertically and horizontally a process for decision-making and communication clearly facilitating strategy, competitive intelligence, and event management initiatives such that the entire organization acts in concert, not as a combination of silos that are held together only by a common corporate name.

Successful demonstration of the ability to execute the event management aspect of business continuity, under simulated conditions, will provide a measure of your organization's ability to respond to an actual event. However, as is often the case, there may be long periods of inactivity between simulations. Should an event occur, personnel may find it difficult to respond appropriately. Periodic simulations help your organization maintain a high state of preparedness, assure integration of strategy, competitive intelligence, and event management into business continuity, and serve as validation of business continuity capabilities.

A well-defined and coordinated simulation program should include a variety of proficiency demonstrations with varying degrees of complexity. Simulations can be segregated into categories based on degree of complexity and level of participation, allowing for the application of common terminology throughout the organization. Establishing a tiered simulation process based on complexity, level of participation, intent of the activity, physical locations involved, and other criteria will allow your organization to build an effectively integrated business continuity program.

The first step developing an effective simulation system is to develop parameters for scenarios. This can be accomplished by reviewing strategy, competitive intelligence initiatives, and the assessments that were made as part of the planning process (see chapters 2, 4, 5, 6, and 7), and maintaining files on current events.

An effective scenario consists of four key elements:

- **Viable story line.** The story that you are going to tell must be viable. The scenario events must be realistic, could or have occurred, are based on fact, and present a challenge to your organization's business continuity. For example, I developed a scenario "7 Minutes to Chaos" that involved a series of terrorist actions. The acts occur as a coordinated effort on the part of the terrorists. The goal of the scenario is to create an environment for issue identification by the participants. I further challenge the participants by asking them to put themselves into decision-making roles that are not common for them. The goal is to create an understanding of the need for integrated continuity with external organizations

- **Realistic timelines.** Your scenario timeline should not have unrealistic time jumps. The use of unrealistic time jumps often throws the participants into confusion and results in lessening the effect of the scenario. Events should be timed so the participants have the opportunity to identify issues and to discuss actions. You should also monitor the realism of participant responses. For example, if you know that an action would take several hours to complete, you should not let the participants off the "hook" by allowing them to move on in the scenario as if the action was complete

- **Applicability to the organization.** The scenario should be applicable to the organization. To run a scenario focusing on events that have no effect or, at best, indirect effects on an organization, is counterproductive. You can achieve success with indirect scenarios if they have a direct impact on an organization. For example, "7 Minutes to Chaos" has indirect effects on the participants in that the events do not directly target their organization per se. The events do, however, require the participants to assess the impact on their organization and its ability to continue business

- **Measurable and observable outcomes.** Creating a scenario for a simulation that cannot be resolved is very simple and can achieve great negative results—so negative that the participants will not participate in future simulations! You should always seek to create scenarios having measurable and observable outcomes. By measurable and observable, I mean that the objectives are clearly stated and can be evaluated against a set of standards. This is important, as the participants need to have a feedback mechanism providing consistent evaluation over time

Simulation scenarios can be structured in many ways. I prefer to use PowerPoint type presentations for smaller groups. The presentation can be orchestrated effectively by manipulating the timing of the slides. As the simulation scenario grows in complexity and participants, I often employ a simulation team to develop, implement, and evaluate performance. This team can be composed of members of the organization who fill roles that are staff support roles. This methodology allows individuals not in primary decision-making roles to develop an understanding of the thought processes of those who are in those roles. It also facilitates the development of expertise in depth for the organization. Executives travel to such an extent today that having decision-making expertise deep into the organization is becoming a "must," not a luxury.

An example of the first type of scenario—the simulation scenario—follows. I was working with a client in New York City who is in the financial services sector. When I was presenting some training material to the executives, I used as an example the *Exxon Valdez* incident. At the break I was told that I should use examples relating more to their industry. Further discussion revealed that the audience could not make the connection between their business continuity (event management) efforts and what had happened in Alaska with the *Valdez* event.

I drew them in during the next session by asking eight questions. First, I asked if they felt that decision-making—the management function—was important. They readily agreed, citing many examples of the decisions they would have to make in order to deal with a business disruption. Next, I asked if they felt that planning, both strategic and tactical, was important. Again, they readily agreed, citing examples of the planning issues they would be faced with in the event of a business disruption. I moved to the third question and asked if they thought that operations were a concern; we had been discussing operational impacts, prevention of cascading effects, and other operations-related issues. Everyone agreed. Then I asked if logistics was an important issue. "Yes," was the response. I then asked my fifth question, is finance important? They all agreed and cited examples of cost-tracking issues, cost accounting, and other related processes for which financing would be responsible. I asked if administration was an area they would consider important. They agreed, citing that personnel, altered work schedules, and other issues would be an administrative function. I asked if infrastructure would be an area they would be concerned with. Again the answer was yes. My eighth and last question was if external relationships would be an area that they would have to address. Again, the answer was yes.

I proceeded to summarize the information we had just discussed on a flip chart and pointed out these were the exact issues that Exxon had to deal with during the *Valdez* event. I also pointed out there were lessons to be learned from this—one of which was despite the fact that Exxon was in an entirely different industry did not mean that the functions Exxon had to execute during the *Valdez* event were any different than the functions my client would have to execute in response to an event.

My point is that the triggering event becomes less important than how your organization responds, manages, and recovers from the event. This is not to say the triggering event is not of significance. The event triggering your response is important because at that point your strategy (mission, vision, values) and competitive intelligence initiatives have been violated. The success of your event response, management, and recovery activities will dictate how strategy and competitive intelligence will be reshaped. There are many lessons to be learned from other industries and the events they have experienced. And, while each event serves to shape the industry sector that it occurs in, as business sectors become more interdependent and interlaced, an event that would appear to have little relationship to another sector can have great potential impact. The lesson to be learned is to look for the wisdom from how events are responded to, managed, and recovered from.

The eight questions I asked my client may be useful as an analysis template. I have summarized them in Table 10-6. You may find this table useful as a way to "kick-start" your thinking the next time you hear of an event in a non-related business sector and think "Well, that could not have any impact on *our* business." The table is in blank form and uses a hypothetical event as an example of how to draw value from the experience of other business sectors.

Area	What went well?	What went poorly?	Lessons to be learned?
Management			
Planning			
Operations			
Logistics			
Finance			
Administration			
Infrastructure			
External relations			

Table 10–6 Assessing Events by Organization Sector

HYPOTHETICAL EVENT SUMMARY

- A utility company experiences a large outage as a result of an explosion and fire in a customer's facility.

- The explosion and fire cause the customer's facility to drop its load demand.

- The rapid drop in load demand causes an imbalance to which the utility's SCADA system is unable to respond to quickly.

- The primary substation serving the customer is not able to handle the resultant load reversal and fails.

- This failure begins to cascade throughout the utility's grid, causing the failure of several substations before the event can be brought under control.

- The utility sustains substantial loss of distribution capability.

- The resultant loss of distribution capability causes the closure of two major metropolitan airports.

- The closure of the airports causes flight delays throughout the aviation industry, causing transportation delays in the ground movement of products such as mail, consumer goods, and automobile parts.

- The transportation delays result in several manufacturers having to stop assembly line operations, due to lack of components.

- The assembly line stoppage causes the stock prices of the automobile manufacturers to drop, followed by steel stocks (due to a lack of demand for steel).

- This in turn leads to layoffs that further accelerate the drop in stock prices as consumers begin purchasing less, leaving retail markets to tailspin because of the drop in demand.

- This leads to a drop in the financial services sector's employment as a result of investors fleeing the market.

- Banks begin to see an increase in late payments and loan failures, leading to federal government action to invigorate the market by dropping interest rates.

- The drop in rates leads to more borrowing and higher credit card usage, which leads to more debt.

- The greater debt leads to less tax revenue collected by the government.

- This leads to higher taxes on consumer goods (tobacco, alcohol, fuel).

- Higher prices for consumption leads to less consumption and more unemployment.

You can go on and on from here. What can be learned from this?

Table 10-7 is an example of the type of lessons that can come out of an event appearing not to have any relation to your business sector.

Area	What went well?	What went poorly?	Lessons to be learned?
Management	Decisions were communicated effectively to all levels within the organization	Dependency on technology left decision-makers little option regarding manual override of systems	Manual override of technology is necessary to assure backup operation of systems Information flow to decision-makers must be timely, accurate, and concise for effective decisions to be made
Planning	Event management plan was executed effectively	Inability to institute manual override of technology delayed implementation of plans	Manual override procedure is needed to supplement technology-dependent system operation
Operations	Event was contained without cascading to other parts of the system	Technology dependency affected operations	Manual override capability required as backup for technology base
Logistics	Movement of replacement equipment was accomplished in a timely manner	Stockpiles of equipment were not located in optimum repositories	Assess logistics staging areas and storage locations
Finance	Cost-tracking systems were implemented effectively	Cost containment was affected due to inability to manually override technology	Develop inputs for manual override procedures
Administration	Human resource elements were effectively brought to respond to the event	Communication through callout system could have been better achieved	Revise callout procedure and seek input from user groups
Infrastructure	External infrastructure systems were not affected by event	External infrastructure impacts not adequately assessed	Revise external infrastructure impact assessment procedure
External Relations	Stakeholder groups were identified and communications were tailored to each group	Consistent communications with various stakeholder groups were sporadic	Assess stakeholder groups for identification of communication requirements, revise communications procedure as necessary

Table 10–7 Lessons from an Event Apparently Unrelated to Your Business Sector

"What if" scenarios

The scenario is also a creative tool that can be used for assessment and analysis steps underlying the basic assumptions of the business continuity process.

What would you do if you worked for Enron, WorldCom, Global Crossing, or one of the other companies recently on the front pages? Could you have envisioned the scenario that each of these companies experienced? Would these scenarios have been included in your approach business continuity? If you had executed such a scenario in a simulation, when would you choose to quit the organization, remembering that you have a mortgage to pay and mouths to feed?

In his recent best-selling book *Leading Quietly*, Joseph Badaracco states that larger-than-life heroics are not what really make the world work. Instead, he says, it is the sum of millions of small, yet consequential decisions made by people far from the limelight every day.

Doing the "right thing" for your organization, your colleagues, and yourself can become a complicated balancing act. When would you decide to stay and exert your influence internally in order to build an organization where you want to work? How can a company build a culture of doing the right thing rather than the expedient thing?

Even if your organization is far from the front pages, it is faced with making decisions fraught with ambiguity every day. How your organization manages these decisions can make or break it. Wouldn't you like to better understand how to do the "right" thing?

The process of creating "what if" scenarios is one I often employ when developing the assumptions underlying the business continuity process for an organization. The "what if" scenario is a wonderful tool for analysis and assessment.

Global Vulnerabilities— Local Impacts

At the beginning of this chapter, I wrote that the chapter is intended to help you to develop scenarios your organization can use to answer the "what if" questions that business continuity management planners should be constantly asking. The following discussion is intended to assist you develop a framework for further analysis and for integrating strategy, competitive intelligence initiatives, and event management into a comprehensive business continuity system.

Table 10-8 covers the areas that I feel are going to become or already are issues potentially threatening business and government from a continuity standpoint as defined herein. Unless you can "think globally and act locally" to integrate business continuity vertically and horizontally within the various levels of your organization and your value chain, your organization will be in a reactive versus a proactive mode. Part of thinking globally and acting locally is the process of data fusion and the communication of the resultant product to the appropriate users. The user's responsibility is then to make and communicate decisions regarding the information, and to further the data fusion analysis process.

The table is two-dimensional for ease of presentation. A multi-dimensional table, akin to a Rubrik's Cube to facilitate the data fusion process is perhaps more useful. A multi-dimensional table reflecting your organization's touchpoints, global vulnerabilities, potential local impacts, etc. can be a very useful tool. However, as complexity grows, you have to recognize that the decision-making process can become bogged down, leading to a syndrome called "decision paralysis."

The more fraught with indecision your organization finds itself, the less able it is to act upon the information available from the data fusion process. Your challenge is to find the optimum decision-making model for your organization that incorporates data fusion and enhances the decision-making and communication process for all touchpoints.

The following categories were used to create the table. In order to understand the categories, I have prepared a definition and examples for each:

Global vulnerabilities. Chapter 1 defined vulnerability as a weakness realized. War is potentially a global vulnerability. One can go back to the largest conflict of the Twentieth Century, World War II, and cite the impact of the war. Remember that impact does not equate to devastation. Many countries were not directly involved in the fighting; however, they were impacted as they were vulnerable in some aspect. Terrorism today is seen as a global vulnerability. I would agree that today terrorism is a global vulnerability as it meets the criteria for being defined as a vulnerability. Terrorism potentially can occur anywhere today. It takes many forms and has the potential for its effects to be felt on a worldwide basis. Famine, global weather, technology changes—all present potential global vulnerabilities. The key to determining global vulnerabilities for your organization is to assess them and their effects on your organization and its value chain, then prioritize them, based on local impacts. If your organization does not operate in Colombia, for example, kidnapping will be less of a concern, unless your organization realizes this vulnerability elsewhere and can use the data from Colombia to reduce your exposure to potential kidnap vulnerabilities in the areas where your organization operates.

Local impacts. Once you establish a list of prioritized global vulnerabilities, you need to begin an assessment of their local impact on your organization, e.g., if another OPEC oil embargo occurred, what would be the impact (near- and long-term) on your organization? Realize that OPEC can institute a global embargo; however, because OPEC has become dependent on the revenues from the oil and gas they produce and because the world economy is much changed since the last oil embargo, the local impact of an embargo will have as many ramifications for the ones conducting the embargo as it will for those under embargo.

Once local impacts are determined, categorized, and prioritized, consequence assessments and consequence management plans can be developed. However, before the consequence management plans can be developed, it would be wise to communicate the consequence assessments as applicable throughout the organization and the value chain. Keep in mind the competitive intelligence and strategy implications for your organization as you determine the communication of this information.

Data source(s). Identifying and assessing the reliability of data sources are key processes in determining consequences. How reliable are the data sources? How many data sources do you need to assure that the information is valid? How do you communicate the information gained from the data source? What is the assessment criteria employed to determine the consequences for your organization? All of these and many more questions need to be answered.

Touchpoints. One must carefully assess global vulnerabilities and their local impacts on all of the touchpoints within the organization. Determining the priority of touchpoints is one of the challenges you need to address as you determine strategy, competitive intelligence, and event management initiatives. What are the consequences to the value chain and how can they be minimized? What constitutes the criteria for determining a touchpoint and how do you rank order the priority of touchpoints for your organization? This may be one of the more challenging tasks for you. How deep do you go in your analysis of touchpoints?

Decision/action. Making a decision can be an arduous task. For example, in an earlier chapter I cited a table from the *Wall Street Journal's* March 11, 2002 edition. The table points out the quandary that decision-makers have, that on the one hand, there were heightened concerns (*i.e.*, mail handling) while on the other, there were greater precautions (*i.e.*, reviewing disaster planning documents). The concerns and the precautions did not correlate. This can lead to decision paralysis, where no decision can be made because the criteria critical to the decision do not correlate to enable the decision to be turned into action.

Adjust. Once a decision has been actualized (turned into action), you have to be prepared to adjust accordingly. It is the principle of action and reaction—"for every action, there is an opposite and equal reaction." The point is that you have to maintain an awareness of the consequences of the actions you take based on your decisions. The actions can only be as good as the decisions. The decisions can only be as good as the information that you have (data fusion), and the information is only as good as the sources that you choose to use.

Responsible entity. Someone or some portion of the organization has to be responsible for ownership of the process. As I see it, this is a central coordinating authority or clearinghouse for information input and intelligence output. Where you choose to place responsibility will influence the tone of the intelligence output. For example, a chief information officer may have a tendency to focus on technology aspects, whereas a chief security officer may blend in more human elements. I often find it necessary to have a champion at a very high level in the organization. This can accomplish a lot. For one thing, you will have high-level ownership of the process. For another, it enables the integration of strategy, competitive intelligence, and event management initiatives. It also allows for the breakdown of the silo effect.

So, let's take a look at the table and some examples of global vulnerabilities and local impacts. Please note that I have kept the examples as simple as possible so as not to over-complicate the process.

Global Vulnerabilities	Local Impacts	Data Source(s)	Touchpoints	Decision / Action	Adjust	Responsible Entity
Government relations	Regulatory change	SEC Federal register Government regulation	Stakeholders Accountants Officers Employees Legal counsel	Assess audit process Insure Insure controls and compliance	Possible change of business and accounting practices	Chief operating officer
Corporate image	Community outreach programs	Local feedback, PR firms News media Value chain components	Value chain Communities Stakeholders Employees Analysts PR Media firms	Assess marketing initiatives Develop and conduct image survey	Strategy, initiatives to enhance image	Vice president public relations
Banking and finance	Access to capital	Banking industry Audit data Accountants Lenders Credit rating agencies	Creditors Suppliers Vendors Stakeholders Regulators Employees Customers	Refinance debt at favorable rates Reduce loan exposure	Debt to equity ratio Increase cash reserves Initiate stock buy back plan	Chief financial officer
International conflict	Operations in affected areas Operations dependent on affected areas	Media Government sources Local intelligence (company personnel) Entities operating in affected areas Associations	Media relations Government relations Employees Suppliers Customers Other business operations Associations	Prepare for altered work schedules Prepare evacuation plans Find alternate sources for supply, production, etc.	Logistics operations Security policies Expatriate policies Travel policies Value chain system	Chief security officer
Loss of critical infrastructure(s)	Inability to function normally	Utilities Media Government Construction Security entities	Value chain Affected entity Input and output Relationships Employees	Identify infrastructure and determine alternate sources	Production supply on hand Work schedules	Chief logistics officer

Table 10–8 Global Vulnerabilities—Local Impacts

The simple example above gives you the essence for the top-level assessments that can be accomplished. You also get an idea of the potential complexity and levels of detail necessary to assure continuity. You can also see the necessity for seamless vertical and horizontal communications to all touchpoints. You should also realize that this is a moving target, constantly in need of assessment and adjustment to assure that business continuity is maintained and that the organization and its value chain remain resilient.

We have to realize that the global nature of business today affects just about every facet of our lives. A former US first lady and a former president of the US coined the phrases, "global village" and "a thousand points of light." These have become reality: A seemingly insignificant event anywhere in the world can have a global impact. This may sound trite, but we see it time and again. The key is to be able to identify the event, quickly assess its potential impacts, and adjust accordingly.

Concluding Thoughts

I am on the mailing (e-mail) list for *The Harvard Business Review*. The *Review* recently e-mailed me several offerings for article reprints that were interesting and appropriate for inclusion in this chapter. "Charting your Company's Future" led off with the following statement:

> *At most companies, the strategic-planning process involves preparing a large document with data culled from a mishmash of sources and replete with charts, tables, and spreadsheets. It's no wonder so few strategic plans turn into action: Executives are paralyzed by the muddle. Here's a new approach, based not on creating a document but on drawing a picture: a strategic canvas.*

I think that this statement clearly illustrates the theme of this book: Unless we redefine business continuity to include strategy, competitive intelligence initiatives, and event management as an integrated approach to doing business, executives will continue to experience decision paralysis. As the statement makes clear, the strategic planning process should paint a picture; however, that picture cannot ever be clear unless we utilize the three primary colors—strategy, competitive intelligence, and event management. For as with the traditional primary colors—red, blue, and yellow—an entire palate can be created, enabling you to see all the tones available.

"The Heart of Change" described "real-life stories of how people change their organizations," and is authored by John P. Kotter and Dan S. Cohen.

> *Kotter and Cohen say the key to effecting meaningful, lasting change lies less in making people think differently, and more in making them feel differently. And they maintain that this appeal to the heart—not the mind—is what compels people to alter their behaviors in the often radical ways that significant change demands.*

By redefining business continuity, I have attempted to get to your heart—to create passion for a way of doing business, and not just adjuncts to the business that your organization does. Integration of strategy, competitive intelligence, and event management into business continuity requires passion. I often hear from traditional business continuity planners that their product is viewed as an adjunct to the business—at best, a necessary evil; at worst, a useless exercise to comply with standards of care or regulatory requirements. Senior management must embrace the process of business continuity as a way of doing business—effectively transforming the business and resulting in resilience, growth, and ultimately, survival.

Another article was entitled, "Fluid Strategies." It started out by offering the question, "How do you move with the power of disruptive change—not against it?" and then answered the question thusly: "Replace rigid formulas with fluid strategies that you redirect as the disruption's stages unfold."

I would say that this aptly describes the redefinition of business continuity. However, if we do not foster the ability to identify potentially disruptive situations, "disruptive change" becomes a part of business continuity, and events will constantly overtake the organization. We will be in a constant state of reactivity, with events controlling the organization, instead of the organization adjusting to events in a proactive and controlled manner. By "controlled" manner, I do not imply rigidity. I see flexibility; or, as the *Harvard Business Review* states, "fluid strategies that you redirect as the disruption's stages unfold."

Lastly, "Strategy: Separating the Essential from the Expendable," states:

> *Today's business leaders are stretched, compelled by shareholders to seek new growth opportunities while simultaneously pressed to hew to their core. Management experts agree that focusing on the core is critical to a company's strategic success, yet they concede that defining the core can be tough.*

"When we survey management teams, I'm always surprised by how much people can vary on this," notes Boston-based Bain & Company management consultant Chris Zook. "Nevertheless, the company must identify its core if leadership is to craft a strategy that effectively focuses the company's efforts." Identifying the "core of business continuity" is integrating strategy, competitive intelligence, and event management initiatives. We discussed "global vulnerabilities and local impacts" in this chapter. I have purposefully stayed away from getting too focused on specific details regarding vulnerabilities. The reason for this is that each organization will have a different perspective when assessing identified vulnerabilities. To provide a cookbook or template would be too restrictive and potentially misleading. Included were examples of two scenario types that I have found useful for the development and validation of business continuity processes. Also included was a discussion of a methodology for data fusion.

As with previous chapters, this chapter is intended to redefine business continuity thinking. By reading this chapter, you should be able to apply the concepts discussed here to further integrate your organization's business continuity process. Key to that process is to communicate intelligence (information transformed into usable knowledge) on the importance of business continuity throughout all levels of your organization and its value chain.

References

Abagnale, Frank W. *Catch Me If You Can*, 1980
———*The Art of the Steal*, 2001

Bararacco, Joseph. *Lead Quietly*

De Becker, Gavin. *The Gift of Fear*, 1997
———*Fear Less*, 2002

Harvard Business Review, "Charting Your Company's Future"
———Fluid Strategies

Huffington, Arianna. *How to Overthrow the Government*, 2000

Kotter, John P., Dan S. Cohen. Harvard Business Review, The Heart of Change

Lake, Anthony. *6 Nightmares*, 2000

Mitroff, Ian, I., "Avoid 'E3' Thinking," *Management General*, 1998
———"Smart Thinking for Crazy Times: The Art of Solving the Right Problems," 1998

Mulgan, Geoff. *Connexity: How to Live in a Connected World*, 1997

Sikich, Geary W. Logical Management Systems, Corp. AUDITRAK^{tm} Diagnostic Assessment Program (www.logicalmanagement.com)

———Logical Management Systems, Corp. (www.logicalmanagement.com), LMS CARVER Touchpoint Analysis Diagnostic Program, 2000

———"Silent War: Violence in the Workplace," 5th Annual Seminar on Crisis Management and Risk Communication, American Petroleum Institute, 1994

———"Managing Transition: Workplace Violence and Crisis Media Management," 1999

———"Strike and Workplace Disruption Planning Guidelines," American Society for Industrial Security, 1999

———"Demonstrating Proficiency: Establishing and Maintaining Performance Standards to Validate Your Crisis Management Program," *Passenger Handling Expert Magazine*, 1999

———"Conducting Effective Tabletop Exercises for Senior Executives," Gas Technology Institute, Emergency Response Conference, May 2001

———"How to Design, Develop and Implement a Successful Drill and Exercise Program," Business Continuity & Contingency Planning Congress, International Quality and Productivity Center, March 17, 2002

Zook, Chris, "Strategy: Separating the Essential from the Expendable," *Harvard Business Review*

Chapter Eleven

CONCLUDING THOUGHTS

Chapter Summary

In this concluding chapter, we will tie together the concepts presented in the previous chapters. This is intended to refresh your memory and help you to pull together the format, structure, and application of your business continuity management plan for various levels of your organization.

Introduction

In this final chapter, I will summarize the highlights of the previous chapters and attempt to bring together the concepts presented and tools provided. We should not think that just because this is the final chapter, it is the end of redefining business continuity. Think of it as the beginning of the next steps for your organization to define business continuity. My

SUMMARY OF TERMS USED IN THE CHAPTERS

Threat
Expression of intent

Hazard
Chance of being harmed

Risk
Probability of occurrence

Vulnerability
Weakness realized

Contingency
Expected action(s)

Consequence
Unexpected results

Business continuity
Strategy, competitive intelligence, event management

Infrastructure
Stand-alone basic structure

Information/communications
Voice, data handling services

Banking and finance
Money handling and financial services

Physical distribution
Utilities (E, G, W) transportation (A, L, S)

Energy
Exploration, production, refining, marketing

Vital human services
Continuity of government, emergency services

hope is that you will take the concepts and thought processes presented here and evolve them to the next level. The tables, figures, and tools presented should be honed and custom-fitted to your unique set of circumstances. This, I hope, will foster the refinement of process and the further integration of business continuity thought into a way of doing business instead, of an adjunct to the business that you do.

Chapter Summaries— Key Concepts

Chapter 1 provided an overview of the potential situations businesses may face in this time of uncertainty. The chapter was designed to provide you with sufficient background material to allow you to focus your efforts when developing your organization's business continuity processes.

We began with some basic assumptions.

- **Assumption #1**—Businesses are complex systems operating within multiple networks
- **Assumption #2**—There are many layers of complexity
- **Assumption #3**—Due to complexity, analysis of event consequences is critical
- **Assumption #4**—Actions need to be coordinated
- **Assumption #5**—Resources and skill sets are key issues

The assumptions were followed by the facts as I viewed them at the time of this writing.

- Events that have been building since the end of World War II, including thousands of terrorist attacks on innocent civilians worldwide, have culminated (so far) in vicious and indiscriminate attacks, first by domestic terrorists, and now by foreign terrorists on the U.S. homeland

- America is not immune from terrorism. Quite the contrary, we are a target-rich environment for both domestic and international terrorists. The stakes are high, and the issues are indeed life, death, and economic survival
- Terrorists are driven to kill people and to destroy property
- All people and all facilities/operations, and therefore all companies, are at risk
- Priority terrorist targets are those of monetary or strategic value, having high human density, and with cultural or symbolic value
- Corporate headquarters of major corporations are prime targets
- Corporations must take responsibility for their survival. Most of what has to be done in the corporate environment must be done by the corporation. Indeed, it is the corporation's responsibility to its people, stakeholders, and the public that relies on its products and services
- Government, on the other hand, must concentrate its efforts on ensuring the protection and preservation of "critical infrastructures" essential to the nation's continued well-being. These infrastructures are:
    - electric power supplies
    - gas and oil
    - telecommunications
    - banking and finance
    - transportation
    - water supply systems
    - emergency services
    - continuity of government

SUMMARY OF TERMS USED IN THE CHAPTERS

Strategy
Mission, vision, values

Competitive intelligence
Acquisition, denial operations

Event management
Response, management, recovery operations

Business continuity
Strategy, competitive intelligence, event management

Knowledge management
Institutional repository of understanding

Time-Critical
Time frame of reference for determining crisis

Classification system
Trigger points for activation of plan

Time-Sensitive
Time frame of reference for determining crisis

Time-Dependent
Time frame of reference for determining crisis

Competitive intelligence
Initiatives to secure a competitive edge in your market

Information
The sum of data collected, information is unprocessed intelligence

owledge management
stematic process for
anaging information
ansformation

elligence life-cycle
ollect, collate, analyze,
lidate, distribute, and
ntrol information

ounterintelligence
perations undertaken
deny information
competitors

UMINT
uman intelligence

risis communications
ommunication under duress

takeholders
ntities with a vested interest
your organization

ata mining
nalysis technique for very
arge databases

nowledge
amiliarity, awareness,
nderstanding

nowledge base
Organized structures of
nformation

Knowledge management
Process of managing and
presenting information

- Corporate America must act now to make key assets (human resources, information resources, equipment, and facilities) unattractive targets for terrorists. Failure to do so is to be vulnerable to an attack

- An "integrated" approach to business continuity will provide the most effective use of resources, facilitate risk reduction, and minimize the potential disruption to the complex network structure of modern business

Based on the stated assumptions and facts, I projected some short- and long-term trends and organized a look at the future into the following areas:

- Human factors
- Infrastructure
- Capital assets (facilities, equipment, etc.)
- Intangible assets (knowledge)
- Value chain (domestic, foreign)
- Technology

Chapter 1 concluded with some thoughts regarding the foundation for business continuity.

In chapter 2, I discussed the vulnerabilities of our critical infrastructures and what can be done to reduce your enterprise's exposure to disruption should one of the critical infrastructures become impaired or suffer degradation sufficient to cause a crisis within your organization.

The critical infrastructures discussed were:

- electric power supplies
- gas and oil
- telecommunications
- banking and finance
- transportation

- water supply systems
- emergency services
- continuity of government

The chapter concluded by observing that protection of critical infrastructures cannot be accomplished by large government-sponsored projects.

In chapter 3, a redefinition of business continuity was introduced to include the integration of strategy, competitive intelligence, and event management. This chapter was designed to get readers to start rethinking how we view planning. Topics included:

- Analysis: steps to an effective business continuity process
- Elements of the "integrated" business continuity process
- Competitive intelligence business impacts during an event
- Communicating sensitive information
- Issues analysis: critical factors facing business today

I proposed the following definition for *business continuity*:

> *All initiatives taken to assure the survival, growth, and resilience of the enterprise*

The chapter was intended to build upon your assessment of potential hazards, threats, risks, vulnerabilities, and consequences.

In chapter 4, I introduced the first of three concepts—the identification of time-critical issues. *Time-critical issues* are defined as issues that can cause an immediate "crisis" for your enterprise.

SUMMARY OF TERMS USED IN THE CHAPTERS

Need to know
Essential information for decision making

Nice to know
Information that does not necessarily direct decisions

Scenario
A creative activity simulating potential events

Worst case
The most devastating outcome

Most-likely case
The most likely outcome

Best case
The most preferred outcome

Critical thinking
Ability to scrutinize facts from multiple perspectives

Data fusion
Assembly of data from seemingly unrelated sources

They are also the issues that have the most immediate impact on your enterprise. Several potential time-critical issues were highlighted:

- loss of critical infrastructures
- telecommunications/information systems
- transportation (air, land, water)
- utilities (gas, electric, water)
- energy supply
- critical services
- access denial
- degradation/loss of critical operations
- loss/degradation of operational capability
- loss of electrical supply sources
- loss of telecommunications/information sources
- loss/degradation of buildings/occupancy
- disruption of transportation
- disruption of water supply
- disruption of emergency services

Also introduced were some analysis tools that can be used for the creation of vulnerability assessments. Figure 11-1 depicts the degree of involvement by various levels within an organization over time and respective of the type of event. Level 3, represented as L3 Business Survivability, depicts the executive management level of an organization (or the federal level in the public sector). As can be seen in the figure, L3 will be highly involved in an event that is "time-critical" and its activities will taper off to a monitoring and support role as the event lessens in severity or is categorized as "time-sensitive" or "time-dependent." The decline in direct involvement and move to monitoring and support functions is generally due to the fact that senior executives are too far removed from the event. Level 2, represented as L2 Business Impacts, depicts the business unit level of an organization (or the state level in the public sector). At this level, the focus and concerns are on the immediate support to the affected entity and the prevention of cascading effects from the event. Level 1, represented as L1 Event Response, depicts the hands-on responder level (or the local level in the public sector). At this level, the focus is on mitigating the event, whether it is a fire, explosion, or natural occurrence.

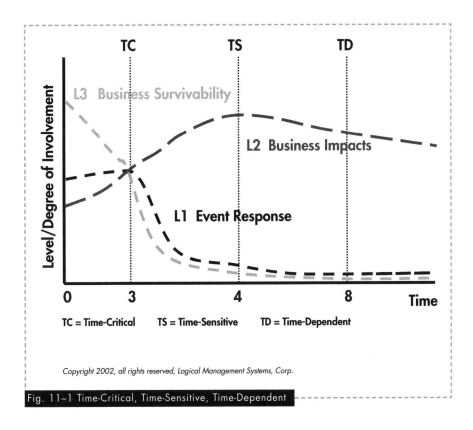

TC   TS   TD

L3 Business Survivability

L2 Business Impacts

L1 Event Response

0   3   4   8   Time

TC = Time-Critical   TS = Time-Sensitive   TD = Time-Dependent

Fig. 11-1 Time-Critical, Time-Sensitive, Time-Dependent

Activity level is very high during the initial stages of an event and declines rapidly as the event is mitigated and the recovery phase is initiated. One should note that the recovery phase generally requires a different organizational composition than the event response organization. This is due to the changed requirements for expertise as the event is mitigated, and new skill sets are required to conduct recovery and restoration.

In chapter 5, we discussed time-sensitive issues, further refining the analysis process. *Time-sensitive issues* were defined as issues that, if left to smolder, will sneak up and cause a crisis for your enterprise. They include, but are not limited to:

- financial issues
- vendor/supplier
- business applications
- human resources and staffing
- legal oversight/documentation

- transition to recovery organization
- recovery operations
- humanitarian assistance
- infrastructure restoration
- information recovery and synchronization
- resumption of critical business functions
- full function restoration
- permanent restoration

In chapter 6, I concluded the discussion of "time" issues by addressing "time-dependent" issues. These included, but were not limited to:

- government relations
- corporate relations
- corporate image
- banking and finance
- assigned relocation sites
- communication systems requirements
- operations systems requirements
- personnel requirements
- documentation of facilities recovery
- assessment of operations requirements
- documents/records required in an emergency
- public sector contacts
- forms and supplies
- associated plans and information
- insurance and risk management plan
- treasury contingency cash plan
- controller's system for tracking recovery expenses
- vendor/supplier/consultant list
- floor space alternatives outside main office
- records planning, storage, and retrieval

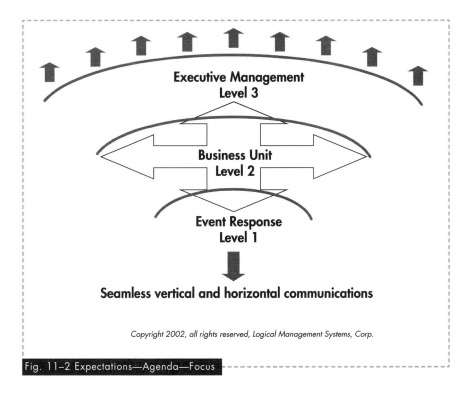

Copyright 2002, all rights reserved, Logical Management Systems, Corp.

Fig. 11–2 Expectations—Agenda—Focus

Chapter 7 presented the business continuity management cycle. This chapter offered an approach to tying together the elements for an organization's business continuity processes. Included were examples of an "integrated" business continuity management plan. Figure 11-2 depicts the various levels within an organization in a simplified form. Level 1, Event Response, is and should be focused on the mitigation of the event. The expectations at this level are for support from above and coordination with entities that support the event mitigation process. The agenda at this level is also fairly straightforward. It is to mitigate the event, minimize the damage and downtime, and ensure the safety of those responding to the event. The focus, as would be expected, is very narrow. At this level, we are focused on the event and what it will take to mitigate the event. In the private sector and public sector, this is commonly referred to as the first response or first responder level.

As we move to the next level, depicted as Level 2 Business Unit (substitute state for public sector readers), we see that the arrows are pointing to all four quadrants of the compass. This is due to altered expectations, agenda, and focus. The expectations at this level are for communication from the affected entity and non-affected entities. This level is also working diligently (we hope) to prevent the event from cascading throughout the organization and its value chain. The agenda is much more complex and involves more data fusion, information sharing, and broader-based decision-making. The focus is vertical as well as horizontal.

At Level 3, Executive Management (read as federal level for public sector), the expectations, agenda, and focus are almost completely 180° from Level 1. This is partially due to the distance from the event in most cases. It is also due to the vastly different agenda that is encountered at this level. The arrows are pointed outward in the figure to depict the focus on the various stakeholders that must be addressed. The expectations at this level are for accurate, timely, and concise communications enabling the communication of critical information to the stakeholders. The agenda is very broad based and encompasses elements of the business that are remote from the event site, the continuation of business activities, and the impact on the value chain.

Chapter 8 presented some thoughts on the ways your organization can limit its exposures to potential situations that may develop into a "crisis". This chapter investigated the value of competitive intelligence collection prior to and during an event. Figure 11-3 highlights the six key questions that I ask clients when we are embarking on an engagement creating a business continuity process for them.

STRATEGY:
What are we committed to?

CONCEPT OF OPERATIONS:
How will we fulfill these commitments?

STRUCTURE:
Do we have an organization that serves our needs?

RESOURCE MANAGEMENT:
How will we manage our resources?

CORE COMPETENCIES:
What skills do we expect from our organization?

PRAGMATIC LEADERSHIP:
How will we optimize authority, decision-making, workflow, and information sharing?

Fig. 11-3 Six Key Questions

I introduced and discussed the three spheres of concern that today's executives have:

- sphere of responsibility
- sphere of influence
- sphere of interest

The chapter concluded with some suggestions on how one can ensure that all levels within the organization are involved in the business continuity process.

In chapter 9, I discussed knowledge management and effective communications concepts, introducing the term *data fusion*—the bringing together of diverse and sometimes seemingly unrelated bits of information to make a complete picture for decision-making. Figure 11-4 depicts the complexity of the data fusion process. It also shows how this complexity can be organized for effective decision-making and the breaking down of information and activity silos. The chapter was intended to help you to identify knowledge sources, establish knowledge management systems, and identify stakeholder groups that you have to communicate with, and which are key to your organization's survival.

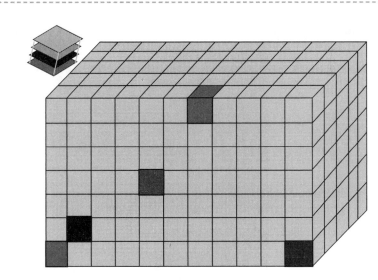

Fig. 11–4 Data Fusion

In chapter 10, scenarios were introduced for future crisis situations. Included were examples of scenarios that can be applied to assess the adequacy and effectiveness of an organization's approach to business continuity. The scenarios included, but should not be limited to:

- government relations
- corporate relations
- corporate image
- banking and finance
- international conflict
- loss of critical infrastructures
- operational events
- terrorism
- workplace violence

I introduced two basic types of scenarios that I employ. These are:

Simulation scenarios. Simulation scenarios are commonly used to validate the event management plan facilitate the development of strategy and competitive intelligence initiatives.

"What if" scenarios. "What if" scenarios are commonly used during the analysis and impact assessment phase to determine possible vulnerabilities and consequences based on identified threats, hazards, and risks.

The chapter concluded with a look at what is being written by others and the potential applicability to business continuity thought process.

The Age of Uncertainty?

We are destined to repeat mistakes unless we learn from them and change our behavior. Once we determine a mistake, we need to change our behavior so that we do not repeat it. As we think about the future, we must look at the past, assess our course, and, if need be, alter and adjust that course.

Flexibility and nimbleness will be two future factors that determine success. Flexibility and nimbleness must have a solid foundation in order to be deployed. The solid foundation, I believe, is the redefining of business continuity to integrate strategy, competitive intelligence, and event management into a way of doing business.

Successful organizations always seem to be able to be one step ahead, in part, due to superior communications and information sharing. I discussed the need for seamless vertical and horizontal communication throughout the organization and its value chain. In order to achieve seamless horizontal and vertical communication, common terminology, consistent methodology, sharing of strategy, and competitive intelligence information (on a "need to know" and sometimes on a "nice to know" basis) must be components of the process. But, without an integrated event-management system, these components are only partial contributors to success, growth, and resilience.

We recently conducted a survey with an organizational consulting firm, Cambridge Human Resource Group, Inc., based in Chicago, which revealed that nearly 50% of the responding companies were not prepared for a crisis. This was emphasized by the fact that nearly half of them have neither detailed business continuity plans and/or integrated crisis management plans in place. Of all respondents, 33% had no formal succession plan in place for their senior management team. Even more stunning was that 30% of the respondents were not sure how to define a crisis, while another 36% responded that any form of business disruption would define a crisis for their organization. Of those surveyed, 40% were unable to name three potential crises facing their organizations over the next five years.

Of those companies that currently have plans in place, only 38% indicated that they actually conduct vulnerability audits to determine potential exposures. Of the respondents with crisis plans, 50% had developed the plans within in the last two years. This raises a question in my mind as to the validity of the plans should a crisis situation materialize.

On August 5, 2002, Globalcontinuity.com (www.globalcontinuity.com) published the results of a survey conducted to discover where responsibility for business continuity lies within companies, and whether it was migrating away from the management level up to the boardroom. The results are interesting and revealing. I have summarized them below.[1]

One result of the survey was that 33.9% of the responses reflected that overall responsibility for business continuity was assigned to a board director. This is an interesting statistic. If roughly 34% of companies have assigned a board director the responsibility for business continuity, why do we not see strategy, competitive intelligence, and event management being integrated into a comprehensive business continuity process? Perhaps an answer lies in the perception of business continuity as an afterthought, an adjunct to the business of the organization. Or could it be that business continuity is not viewed as a comprehensive process? Perhaps there are too many "silos" yet to come down? The statistical breakdown in Table 11-1 from the Globalcontinuity.com survey is revealing also.

Board Responsibility for Business Continuity by Region	Percent
United Kingdom	53.9
Canada	40
Austral-Asia	26.2
United States of America	22.4

Table 11–1 Board Responsibility by Selected Countries

The survey gave the following breakdown regarding the board-level responsibility for business continuity.

- 15.1%—chief finance officer/finance director
- 13.2%—chief information officer/chief technology officer/it director
- 9.8%—chief executive officer
- 8.8%—chief operating officer/operations director
- 7.3%—managing director
- 5.4%—vice president
- 1.9%—president
- 1.5%—chairman
- 37%—other director titles

In the companies where business continuity is not a board director post, the survey results were:

- 50.9%—senior managers
- 23.2%—middle managers
- 14.5%—non-board directors

- 7.5%—low-level managers
- 3.1%—administrators
- 0.9%—external consultants

While these results are interesting, they do not reveal representation on a departmental or business unit level (*i.e.*, human resources, information technology, operations, etc.). It is revealing to note that 3.1% were listed as "administrators." Assuming that administrators represent the human resource functions, one has to question the depth of the business continuity plans, especially in light of how I have redefined the term. I say this not to demean administrators, but to acknowledge that they are often overlooked in the broader scheme of things in the organization.

The survey commented on the statistical differences, citing:

> *It may indicate that business continuity is taken more seriously as a holistic discipline in the UK than in other countries. The US has historically concentrated more on disaster recovery aspects of business continuity than UK companies have. Disaster recovery does not require the same in-depth knowledge of the day-to-day working of the company as holistic business continuity does, hence offering one possible reason for the much higher number of UK companies passing responsibility for BC up to director level.*

Globalcontinuity.com asked whether respondents felt that business continuity would become a board-level position in their company in the future. The results indicated that more than half of the respondents (52.8%) felt that business continuity would become a board-level position/responsibility. This is somewhat heartening and reminds one of the early days of the chief information officer (CIO): When the position of CIO was first beginning to make inroads into companies, many felt that it would never rise to a board-level responsibility as it is today. Learn from your mistakes and do not repeat them! Many respondents felt that the elevation of business continuity to the boardroom would take place between one and five years from hence.

Finally, the Globalcontinuity.com survey asked how often business continuity issues were referred to the board for discussion (Table 11-2).

Business Continuity Issues Referred to Board for Discussion	Percent
Never	17
Infrequently	50.1
Frequently	21.9
Always	9.9
Did not answer the question	1.2

Table 11–2 How Often are Business Continuity Issues Referred to the Board?

It appears that the United Kingdom leads the way in moving business continuity to a board-level responsibility. I think that all readers of this book should encourage their management and board to take a serious look at the wide range of threats, risks, and hazards that imperil organizational survival, and remind them that it is the responsibility (morally and ethically) of senior management and board members to focus on ensuring the survival, growth, and resilience of the enterprise.

We cannot continue to view business continuity in the way that we have. Business continuity must become an integral and integrated way of doing business. Executives around the world should be asking themselves some serious questions about their commitment to their business' future. A lack of senior executive and board-level recognition of the importance of "integrated" business continuity can only lead to greater vulnerabilities and more severe consequences should a disruptive event occur. Organizations that approach business continuity from the traditional silo perspective rather than recognizing it as an integration of strategy, competitive intelligence, and event management may reap the windfall that Enron, Global Crossing, WorldCom, and others have experienced. The results of the Globalcontinuity.com survey and the survey that we recently performed would seem to indicate that this is, unfortunately, still the case.

The Value of Information Sharing

An example of the value of information sharing was a June 27, 2002 information summary (or INFOGRAM) published by the National Information Protection Center (NIPC: (202)323-3205, Fax: (202)323-2079; http://www.nipc.gov/incident/cirr.htm).

The INFOGRAM discussed the benefits derived from the dedicated and trusted two-way information sharing between NIPC and the emergency services sector (fire, emergency medical services, law enforcement). These organizations were urged to cooperate by providing information about suspicious contacts, hazards, threats, attacks, and vulnerabilities. They were also encouraged to submit security "best practices." With this cooperation, NIPC is able to assemble information (data fusion), identify patterns, methods, and sources of potential actions directed against the critical infrastructures of the U.S. The following is excerpted from the INFOGRAM:

During the latter part of July, two EMS organizations (one in Pennsylvania and another in Florida) forwarded to NIPC an electronic message they received from a program manager in the Defense, Space and Environment Division, of a company located in Rome, Italy. The message requested information about the application of satellite navigation (e.g., GPS) for ambulance tracking and route guidance. It also inquired about the use of other special equipment for American ambulance operations. Within 72 hours of receiving the first notification with the message from Italy attached, the NIPC completed an investigation and substantiated that the electronic request for information originated from a registered Italian company with legitimate emergency services contracts. Both EMS organizations decided not to comply with the request because of the sensitivity of the information and lack of secure communications.

This episode serves as an example of how information sharing can assist organizations in making decisions regarding critical infrastructures. The INFOGRAM further cited:

The International Criminal Police Organization (Interpol) has conducted investigations of suspected terrorists and other criminals who successfully obtained employment in positions related to community infrastructures. Interpol warns that this is an increasingly attractive option for terrorists seeking access to the critical infrastructures (people, physical entities, and cyber systems) of any community, but especially those in the United States.

Given this warning, how can operators in the U.S. who are responsible for critical infrastructures at the national, state, and local levels not be more vigilant in investigating the background history of all recently hired and new candidates? Of course this assumes that the operators are aware of the information!

Concluding Thought

Speculation regarding "the next crisis" to affect your organization may add excitement for hallway discussions, but securing executive management and board member commitment is critical for assuring business continuity.

In a seminar conducted for the Business Resumption Planners Association in Chicago, I posed the following question to the attendees: "Is business continuity a way of doing business for your organization or is it an adjunct to your business?" I was not surprised by the silence that fell over the room. After a few minutes, one brave soul admitted that business continuity planning is viewed as an adjunct to their organization's business—"a necessary evil," in other words.

The danger of letting this happen is that your organization exposes itself to unnecessary and unknown vulnerabilities. This increases potential liability, because your organization has failed to take prudent and appropriate precautions. *Black's Law Dictionary* defines *constructive knowledge*:

> *If one by the exercise of reasonable care would have known a fact, he is deemed to have constructive knowledge of such fact; e.g. matters of public record*

With all that has been reported, recorded, and institutionalized, can executive management, board members, and employees continue to view business continuity as an adjunct function to business?

NOTES

1. Globalcontinuity.com's conducted a web-based survey and received 690 replies from business continuity practitioners around the world. The U.S. accounted for 44% of the responses. The United Kingdom accounted for 20.4% of the responses. Austral-Asia accounted for 6.1% and Canada accounted for 5.8%.

References

Black's Law Dictionary, definition of Constructive Knowledge

Cambridge Human Resources Croup, Inc. and Logical Management Systems, Corp. (www.logicalmanagement.com), "Survey Results: How Prepared is Your Organization?" July 2002

Globalcontinuity.com Survey Results, "Is Responsibility for Business Continuity moving up in Organizations?" (www.globalcontinuity.com), August 5, 2002

National Infrastructure Protection Center (NIPC) INFOGRAM, June 27, 2002

Sikich, Geary W. 7 Minutes to Chaos, Business Continuity Planners Association, Chicago, July 2002.

————"7 Minutes to Chaos: What Federal, State and Local Responders should expect when dealing with the Business Community," National Institute for Government Innovation, Annual Conference, September 2002

Geary Sikich leads Logical Management Systems, Corp.'s management advisory services consulting services (www.logicalmanagement.com). Prior to founding Logical Management Systems, Corp., in 1985, he served in key management roles for several major consulting and accounting firms. He has functioned as project director and consultant for Fortune 10 and Fortune 100 firms addressing some of the highest profile "crisis" situations throughout the world. Among his many accomplishments, Mr. Sikich is a recognized expert in the field of crisis management planning, crisis containment, and business continuity processes. He is the author of three previous books on crisis management planning:

It Can't Happen Here: All Hazards Crisis Management Planning, published by PennWell Publishing in 1993

The Emergency Management Planning Handbook, published by McGraw-Hill in 1995

The Emergency Management Planning Handbook, Spanish ed., published by McGraw-Hill in 1998

Mr. Sikich has published more than 100 articles, papers, and presentations on crisis management, business continuity, and other management issues. He is a lifetime member of the Association of Former Intelligence Officers. A graduate of Indiana State University, and the University of Texas at El Paso, he regularly presents programs for executives and is recognized internationally as a speaker and symposium leader. Mr. Sikich has lectured on crisis management system design, business continuity processes, identifying and controlling vulnerabilities, risk and threat assessment, regulatory compliance, terrorism, workplace violence prevention, and management decision-making.

INDEX

A

Accessibility determination, 27-28

Accidents/natural events, 25

Account numbers/passwords, 73

Acronyms, xv

Action coordination, 4, 147

Adjustment, 201

Administrative EPIP, 147

Age of uncertainty, 7-12, 151-166, 218-222: technology, 7; business continuity, 7; threat trend assessment, 8-12; protecting your organization, 151-166

Agile restoration, 54-55

Ambiguous warfare, 183

Analysis/integration framework, 198-203: global vulnerabilities, 199, 202-203; local impacts, 200, 202-203; data sources, 200; touchpoints, 200; decision/action, 201; adjustment, 201; responsibility, 201

Anticipated events, xx

Applicability (simulation), 193

Assessment (critical infrastructures), 33-43, 63-69, 86, 127: energy, 34-36; information/communications, 36-37; banking and finance, 37-38; transportation, 38-39; human services, 40-43; areas, 63-69, 86; impact analysis, 127

Assessment areas (business continuity), 63-69, 127: human factors, 63; operations analysis, 63; technology analysis, 64; facilities analysis, 64; equipment analysis, 64-65; infrastructure touchpoints, 65; AUDITRAK™, 66-69; decision-making model, 67-68; disaster exposure rating, 68-69; impact analysis, 127

Assessment areas (time-critical events), 86

Assigning responsibility, 74, 87-88, 152, 201, 215-216, 219-222: survey, 219-222

Assumptions (uncertainty), 3-5, 208: public sector, 5; private sector, 5

AUDITRAK™, 4, 66-69: elements of analysis, 66-67; measure of effectiveness, 66-67; measure of performance, 66-67; data elements, 66-67

F

G

H

I

K

L

M

N

S

T

U

V

W

HERE'S WHAT CUSTOMERS ARE SAYING ABOUT SHOPPING ONLINE AT WWW.PENNWELL-STORE.COM:

"The service was great; I had my order within a few days —
when all other stores didn't have it in stock."
— Scott R., Accokeek, MD

"I was very pleased with the service. Excellent response to my
e-mail inquiring about my order status. I will be ordering from
PennWell again in the near future."
— Chester G., Wilmington, DE

"I couldn't find a couple of items, I left an email, and they
shipped the items as well. The online store is excellent and has
my highest regards and approval."
— Scott E., Ilion, NY

"Being that I haven't ordered online at all in the past, the only
basis I had for the quality and speed of service was the feedback
from friends and relatives. PennWell has certainly made my first
online experience a pleasant one..."
— Hercules R., Westminster, CA

"Already received the order and the invoice — it was quite
user-friendly. Will definitely order again online. Thank you!"
— Brenda P., Denver, CO

What are you waiting for? Shop online today at
www.pennwell-store.com!

**Don't forget to sign up for our e-newsletter
to keep up with our latest titles and offers!**

"Neal Adams does a masterful job in vividly portraying the terrorist danger against the international oil industry."
—Prof. Michael J. Economides, Co-Author of The Color of Oil

"Your book really opened my eyes. I didn't realize how vulnerable the American way of life was because of our great need for oil...the purposed tactical applications you set forth are 'sound' and well thought out."
—Chris Andersen, Sergeant, Houston Police Department

"**Terrorism & Oil** provides a wealth of information on the threats faced by the oil and gas industry as well as solutions to reduce the risk of being targeted."
—Karim H. Vellani, CPP, President of Threat Analysis Group, LLC and author of Applied Crime Analysis.

"**Terrorism & Oil** provided me with information I would not thought of before. It was an easy read and made very good sense."
—Chief Mark Wallace, McKinney (TX) Fire Department and author of Fire Department Strategic Planning.

* * * * * * * * * * * * * * * *

Terrorism & Oil is the first book to take an in-depth look at the oil industry's vulnerabilities to terrorism. Written by Neal Adams, one of the most influential voices in the oil industry, **Terrorism & Oil** delivers a powerful and thought-provoking message to a society addicted to this threatened resource.

Divided into two sections—Education and Action—**Terrorism & Oil** is a rich source of information providing

- a history of terrorism and oil supply disruptions
- valuable production/consumption statistic tables and graphs
- an overview of transportation choke points and infrastructures
- valuable site assessment checklists
- an overview of typical terrorist weapons

Overall, Adams delivers thought-provoking content and draws soundly intelligent conclusions which make **Terrorism & Oil** a valuable must-read for a society facing a new era of terrorism.